POET SHOWCASE

Poet Showcase

An Anthology of New Hampshire Poets

Edited by
Alice B. Fogel and Sidney Hall Jr.

HOBBLEBUSH BOOKS
Brookline, New Hampshire

Hobblebush Books
17-A Old Milford Road
Brookline, New Hampshire 03033
www.hobblebush.com

ISBN: 978-1-939449-1-15
Library of Congress Control Number: 2015953951

Composed in Dante MT Std at Hobblebush Books
Printed in the United States of America

Cover art is a painting by Childe Hassam: *Landscape at Newfields, New Hampshire, 1909*

Just specimens is all New Hampshire has,
One each of everything as in a showcase,
Which naturally she doesn't care to sell.

—from "New Hampshire" by Robert Frost

Acknowledgments

Hobblebush Books gives special thanks to the New Hampshire State Council on the Arts whose website hosted the original Poet Showcase curated by New Hampshire Poets Laureate Patricia Fargnoli and W. E. Butts.

The editors wish to especially thank Kirsty Walker, marketing director and partner at Hobblebush Books, for the many hours it took to herd 117 poets into a book, and deal with all the logistics of permissions and commentaries and bios. It was a major enterprise that only Kirsty could carry off so well. Thanks also to Hobblebush intern Marissa O'Shea for helping with this work. And thanks to the many publishers, big and small, that granted us permission to reprint these poems.

Contents

Introduction

WHY DO WE HAVE SO MANY POETS IN NEW HAMPSHIRE? Is it the long winters of contemplation, the rugged and inspirational landscapes, magic granite particles glittering invisibly in the air? Whatever the reason, life in New Hampshire offers unhurried opportunities for artists to develop a craft that offers—through contemplation and inspiration, as well as observation and ineffable alchemy—a way to give form and language to the experience of our lives.

Not that the poets here would claim to be alike. While all of the poets you'll find in *Poet Showcase* have lived in New Hampshire and many are originally from New England, many others are from cities and countrysides across North America, and some are from other continents. The poets on the official New Hampshire "Poet Showcase" website and in this anthology are drawn from every decade of life—from the second to the tenth. But despite this democratic inclusivity, they do have in common the geographic boundaries they call home, and the practice of poetry to which they have committed themselves.

The original showcase began during Patricia Fargnoli's term as New Hampshire Poet Laureate, which ran from 2006 to 2009. At her request, The New Hampshire State Council on the Arts gave her access to the poet laureate page on its website, in order that she might feature poems by poets from around the state. The poets were chosen by invitation only, but Patricia asked for recommendations from others and made sure to include both the famous and the less famous, the goal being to find and feature poetry by those who were seriously working at the craft, no matter the stage or degree of their literary career. Patricia presented a different poet and poem every two weeks.

As Patricia herself says, "The project was, I felt, important as a way to give recognition and visibility to the many serious poets in New Hampshire. It was extremely rewarding to me to become familiar with a wide variety of poets across the state, to showcase their talents, and to provide this link between them and their potential readers." Patricia showcased over seventy poets during her tenure.

Walter Butts followed Patricia Fargnoli as the next New Hampshire Poet Laureate. He was eager to keep the showcase going, as he felt it helped connect poets in New Hampshire with each other, and helped them gain visibility with readers. He could not have been more right in thinking that it also provided a wonderful place for readers to go for good poetry, and to discover local poets they did not know of, who might even live right in their community. Ever mindful of keeping the site's quality and freshness, Walter invited several writers who had already published on the site to publish again, and also mixed in new ones, adding about eighty more poems to the collection. Walter was not able to finish his term, as he passed away too soon. But his wife, S Stephanie (whose work also appears in the series) says she believes Walter would be pleased that the fruits of his and Pat's labors went to print.

As the current New Hampshire Poet Laureate, it is my wish too to bring wider recognition to our poets, and to bring more readers of all experience levels and affinities to poetry. Hobblebush Books shares this mission, having over the past five years developed the invaluable Hobblebush Granite State Poetry Series that includes works by six of the poets in these pages. As Hobblebush continues to publish poets who are not simply skilled but have, as the publisher puts it, "lifted words into a new realm of spirit that did not exist before," this anthology is a valuable addition to their work.

Of course this survey of contemporary New Hampshire poets, however broad, is not inclusive of every soul in our state who puts pen to paper. And of course the topics covered by our poets are by no means comprehensive here, as there is no end to the possibilities for poetry's content. But a wide range of poetry's usual themes appears in this book in new ways that "did not exist before": war and peace, love and loss, death, age, time, animals and elements, small towns and small moments, the news, the arts, mystery, food, family relationships, God, objects, things we do and things we perceive, and—yes—granite. Surprisingly little about the weather, though. But what are poems really "about"? What these poems, in forms ranging from the lyric to narrative, and including a few prose poems and experimental approaches, are really often "about" is life—and language itself.

One of the added delights of this collection is that each poem is followed by the poet's original commentary about the origin of the poem. We hope you will read the poem first, savoring its images and its sounds and getting the full experience of the poem, and then deepen your understanding of it by reading the commentary. On their own, the commentaries are a fascinating study in the genesis of poems.

My vision for this anthology is that it be treasured, found on bedside tables, living room couches, library shelves, and classroom desks, that it travel from place to place and reader to reader, in backpacks and shoulder bags and on car seats, loaned and shared, dog-eared and discussed, read and reread, inspiring each of us to look up from its pages, peer deeper inside ourselves, and gaze farther outward into the world of New Hampshire and beyond.

—ALICE B. FOGEL, NEW HAMPSHIRE POET LAUREATE
ACWORTH, NEW HAMPSHIRE, JUNE 2015

Note: Although every effort was made to contact every poet who appeared on the Poet Showcase website, unfortunately we failed to reach some of the poets and they could not be included. In cases where the same writer appeared twice on the website, the editors selected just one of that poet's poems, so that the total number of poets appearing in Poet Showcase is one hundred and seventeen.

Poems featured in

Patricia Fargnoli's Poet Showcase

(2006–2009)

Juli Nunlist

VIEWPOINT

If you look
this way and that
you will see things

differently. This way
you see the fisherman
in the blue cap

is holding a net,
in fact he is
mending it,

retying a knot
that has come undone
at one corner.

You imagine the net tonight
filled with the silver gleam
of fish scales

as his boat bumps
against the dock, its deck
luminous with his catch.

But if you look that way,
you see the fisherman is holding
an enormous number

of holes tied together
with string,
and he is trying,

by knotting the corner
to keep one of the holes
from escaping.

What I love in her poem, "Viewpoint," is the way it's pared down to absolute essentials, the impeccable line breaks, the lilt of its language and the twist of perception it contains, how it turns the world inside-out and makes me see and think differently. —*Patricia Fargnoli*

Marie Harris

WESTERN GREBE

Aechmophorous occidentalis
Sun-setting spear-bearer

On any one of his long-strided walks
near the Mandan settlement that first fall,
Meriwether Lewis encountered all manner of shorebirds
and ducks plying the sloughs.
Naturalist, explorer, he shot one of each.
Taxidermist, he sent specimens back East.
Diarist, he described each one shot to the last pinfeather.

I write in my journal
(a letter to you from the West)

. . . the wind that flattens the tall grass prairie
and keeps blackbirds and meadowlarks low,
deafens foraging waterfowl
to my slow advance.

I am seeing for the first time

> *for the first time! imagine!*

long-legged, blue-legged avocets
giddily spinning phalaropes
the thin-necked grebe with its sharp bill and red eye

So would you, reader,
be my correspondent,
my accomplice?

My Jefferson.

→

As I write poems occasioned by, say, a book I've read or places I've visited, I often weave my fascination with birding into the lines. This poem takes that notion even a step further. I was invited to North Dakota and the second gathering of state poets laureate. North Dakota laureate, Larry Woiwode, asked each of us to compose a poem on the occasion of the 200th anniversary of the Lewis and Clark expedition. This was my offering.

Maxine Kumin

NEW HAMPSHIRE, FEBRUARY 7, 2003

It's snowing again.
All day, reruns
of the blizzard of '78
newscasters vying
for bragging rights
how it was to go hungry
after they'd thumped
the vending machines empty
the weatherman clomping
four miles on snowshoes
to get to his mike
so he could explain
how three lows
could collide to create
a lineup of isobars
footage of state troopers
peering into the caked
windows of cars
backed up for white
miles on the interstate.

No reruns today
of the bombings in Vietnam
2 million civilians blown
apart, most of them children
under 16, children
always the least
able to dive
for cover when
all that tonnage bursts from a blind sky.
Snow here is
weighting the pine trees
while we wait for the worst:
for war to begin.

Schools closed, how
the children
love a benign blizzard
a downhill scrimmage
of tubes and sleds. But who
remembers the blizzard
that burst on those other children?
Back then we called it
collateral damage
And will again.

I came to write "New Hampshire, February 7, 2003" out of anguish and fury; it was clear that we were going to invade Iraq, that we had learned nothing from our disaster in Vietnam. And day by day I feel ever more strongly that as poets we have an obligation to society to speak out, to bear witness to the events around us. This poem led me to write the nine torture poems that followed and that will stand as a separate unit in my not-quite-finished manuscript, *Still to Mow*.

W. E. Butts

SUNDAY FACTORY

We walk along the street
Sunday afternoon,
past the stone church, on our way
to visit his place of work.
This is the religion of father and son,
the faith of a boy who's only five,
the factory a blessing of meat and bread,
the big machines still as statues,
an assembly of clocks
to mark the next week's labor.
Here are the instruments of the makers,
their testaments of gears and wheels.
This is where men and women are called
to the daily stations of common task,
and so I stand with my father
in a child's reverent silence.
Tomorrow, he'll enter the loud,
humming chorus of his eight hour shift
to hose down the conveyor belts
so many times his forearms will ache
until they become light as air.
This is when he thinks of the boy
and his schoolbooks, remembers his wife
and her lilac corsage that morning they married.
And he makes what he can from each of these hours
that will, at last, take him home.

"Sunday Factory" is from a recent sequence of poems around the themes of small town America and father/son relationships. I've become increasingly interested in how the past is restored in memory and impacts on the present. Ironically, what's remembered becomes the newly discovered.

Pat Frisella

COUPS DE COEUR
(Wounds to the Heart)

Cardinals at the windows see enemy
    black and white newspapers turn to color
reflections or crimson hills and horses
    for added effect. There's a lot of red now, flames,
in the painting on the wall on the other side of
    blasts, and plasma. On today's front page a van ablaze,
the glass between us and them, and wound
    soldiers in desert camo hauling a white-haired man,
themselves, struggling against an imaginary foe,
    panting, their mouths open, they sprint,
when they run out of real opponents to fight;
    two of them hurry this frail being from doom,
I want to save them from each other, save them from
    children wounded by bombs, burned,
themselves, from this lust and smudge of feathers,
    and a man holding his blood-soaked thigh against pulp,
limp bodies with broken necks. I pull lace
    radiating from where legs have been; I want to save them,
curtains shut and they quiet, and singing, begin to gather
    from each other. I want to save them from themselves,
horsehair and dry grass for their nests, to plump and to redden.

I struggle sometimes with trying to maintain awareness of the terrible news in
current events and awareness of all that is still beautiful—what Brecht was speak-
ing of when he said it is hard to write about trees when the forest is full of police.
This poem uses a form I learned from listening to Maggie Dietz at PEA one time.
She spoke of weaving together two poems that want to be together but did not
arrive together, and that is what I have done here—alternating lines from one
with lines from the other, with some final tweaking to smooth out the rough
spots. If you read all the odd lines you get a poem and if you read all the even
lines you get another poem, and yet they come together. An internal struggle.

Donald Hall

NAMES OF HORSES

All winter your brute shoulders strained against collars, padding
and steerhide over the ash hames, to haul
sledges of cordwood for drying through spring and summer,
for the Glenwood stove next winter, and for the simmering range.

In April you pulled cartloads of manure to spread on the fields,
dark manure of Holsteins, and knobs of your own clustered with oats.
All summer you mowed the grass in meadow and hayfield, the mowing machine
clacketing beside you, while the sun walked high in the morning;

and after noon's heat, you pulled a clawed rake through the same acres,
gathering stacks, and dragged the wagon from stack to stack,
and the built hayrack back, uphill to the chaffy barn,
three loads of hay a day from standing grass in the morning.

Sundays you trotted the two miles to church with the light load
a leather quartertop buggy, and grazed in the sound of hymns.
Generation on generation, your neck rubbed the windowsill
of the stall, smoothing the wood as the sea smooths glass.

When you were old and lame, when your shoulders hurt bending to graze,
one October the man, who fed you and kept you, and harnessed you every morning,
led you through corn stubble to sandy ground above Eagle Pond,
and dug a hole beside you where you stood shuddering in your skin,

and lay the shotgun's muzzle in the boneless hollow behind your ear,
and fired the slug into your brain, and felled you into your grave,
shoveling sand to cover you, setting goldenrod upright above you,
where by next summer a dent in the ground made your monument.

For a hundred and fifty years, in the pasture of dead horses,
roots of pine trees pushed through the pale curves of your ribs,
yellow blossoms flourished above you in autumn, and in winter
frost heaved your bones in the ground—old toilers, soil makers:

O Roger, Mackerel, Riley, Ned, Nellie, Chester, Lady Ghost.

When I came back to live in New Hampshire in 1975, I was full of everything that I remembered from my childhood summers spent haying with my grandfather on this farm. One of the matters I remembered most clearly was the series of work horses, and after I moved back to this house I wrote "Names of Horses" to celebrate and memorialize them.

L. R. Berger

NOTES FROM EAGLE ISLAND
(Excerpts)

Moon as scimitar.

The hour of last light.

I scavenge for the revelation
lurking in every form.

The darkening woods
calls you to declare
what you believe in—

I took the wrong trail
at the crossroad.

My body is torn
between the fear of being
lost, and the work
of finding my way home—

between the impulse to run
and the impulse to kneel.

     ★ ★ ★

We are children of these accidental, but
nevertheless, communions.

The loon wakes me. Sound of one voice
and another that answers,
tremolo saturating the August air
for miles.

I haul myself up, wooden bucket full
from the well.

On neighboring islands, others
are drawing themselves
half-willingly from sleep

to hear the wailing of two birds, a calling
we have no choice but to share in the night

blackened as the glass chimney
on the kerosene lamp, the wick
gone too long untrimmed.

This poem is an excerpt from "Notes from Eagle Island," a series of twenty-six poems that was written over three years. The poems first emerged, literally, as hundreds of scraps of images and conversations collected in notebooks while visiting Eagle Island in Maine. I had worked for many years studying and writing about Rachel Carson. Carson's early writing life was devoted to introducing readers to the biology of the sea, and in one of her letters she said, "I wanted to take the seashore out of the realm of scenery." These poems chronicle my experience of gradually opening to deeper encounters with the sea and life of the island, and to being opened.

My imagination was engaged over a long period of time with the demands of this series: how would I ever find any cohesion or discover the necessary form for these hundreds of images? It was work that taught me a great deal about faithful persistence and openness in the face of seeming chaos and uncertainty. This is often true with poems, but I had never undertaken something of this magnitude that required sustaining myself in the uncertainty for so long. Slowly, the scraps began to speak to each other, then to me, and through me. My hope, of course, is that the poems now speak to others, offering something approaching companionship.

Meg J. Petersen

BRINGING DOWN THE CEILING

Seek out the shadowed slits into which
the metal blade might fit.
Find the point of pressure
and steady yourself.
Exploit the hidden fault lines
in the plaster.
Brace your weight and push—
not strong, but cautious,
as if to pump brakes on glare ice.
Expose yet another row
of bare wooden slats.
Try not to breathe
until the dust settles.

Remember how we go about our lives
believing the ceiling, the walls, the frames
will hold
And as the pieces crack and plummet,
as the heavy horsehair plaster falls,
splits and drops like strange rain,
lands with a thud you will hear
in your dreams,
remember all those times the metaphor
arrived too perfect to name, too whole
to swallow, and wonder
if you can ever know you love anything again
until you have split apart its seams.

This poem came out of the quite literal experience of having to take down a
horsehair plaster ceiling. I had a lot of time to hone the images as I worked at it
over the course of a weekend. I thought about a story my friend Robert Miller
wrote in which he used a falling ceiling as a "metaphor too perfect to name."
The last line emerged in revision, surprising me with how it made me rethink
the whole experience.

Laura Davies Foley

SYRINGA

I thought I would see a flutter of feathers,
a streak of blood,
maybe some bones.
The fox in the night would be satisfied,
or the hawk, or the eagle and I would lean against a tree
and I would feel the loss, the empty space.
Instead, she greets me from a spot far off on the lake.
She stretches out her broken wing
as if to question my intention,
my coming, my watching.
Her body shines in the copper light.

It is difficult for both of us,
the endless floating in dark water,
the waiting eyes,
the pale, cold sky
and ice.
Every day the clutching branches of ice.

And I have come to love her. It is difficult,
the ice like lace, the glow of her neck
as she arches back upon herself,
the desolation of the sky, and joy,
the wild joy that blossoms toward us in the dark.

Syringa is a bird with a broken wing who survives long winters on the edges
of a frozen pond in New England. She is joined each spring and fall by other
birds who stop for a while and then fly off to their summer breeding grounds in
Canada, or their winter shelters to the south.

   She seemed to me a wild friend, appearing one day near the woods where I
walk. I felt that seeing her was a privilege, and I thought I was going to experi-
ence the privilege of watching her die.

At one point early on I pitied her, and requested help from a wildlife agency. They said they could not fix the wing and so advised euthanasia. I decided to do nothing. That was years ago.

In some ways the bird has been my teacher, constant and serene, her flawed wing no greater hindrance to freedom than the normal flightlessness we all experience when we are awake enough to notice.

I call her Syringa because I like the cadence of the word, its soft swan sounds, its evocation of lilacs, exotic trees and fragrant, faraway places. But she is just a simple goose. Quite ordinary . . .

Parker Towle

HOOKING RUGS AND ICE-FISHING

He volunteered with a dying patient
expecting to go through the five stages of grief
at the first meeting. Instead
she talked about hooking rugs:

the needle, the thread, the cloth,
the rhythmic movement of the hands.
He tried other matters in conversation—
she talked of hooking rugs.

On the next visit she spoke of intricacies
and hardships of ice-fishing that her husband
had done before his death. Week after week,
hooking rugs and ice-fishing.

Angered, he said to friends,
"I can't go on with this
interminable hooking rugs
and ice-fishing."

One day as they sat
in the hospital cafeteria,
she going on, he bored and vexed
with hooking rugs and ice-fishing

the room
went silent, air turned
a luminous shade of green, hooking
rugs and ice

fishing stopped. She leaned over and said,
"I could not have done this
without you,"
then on again with hooking rugs

and ice-fishing. Soon after she died. At the funeral
relatives said to him, "Thank you,
all she ever spoke about
was you."

This story, carried in hospice practice in the "ballad tradition" I presume, was
told at the Frost Place during the festival some years ago by Don Sheehan, our
first director (for twenty-six years or so until 2006), as an illustration of the sly
and unexpected messages that language carries. When Don's talk was over I sat
in the barn and scribbled it down as fiercely as I could, no doubt adding one of
many new spins, enacting the "creative" process we call memory.

John Perrault

AT THE HOME

Mother opens up the blinds
on her two windows,
finds the locks and lifts—

nearly blind at ninety-four,
she hears the finches first
before she spies them,
flitting outside the screen—

little flashes of red
blinking in the ivy bush,
lighting up the leaves.

Leaning on her walker
she whispers through the mesh,
just like in confession,
so as not to wake her neighbors:

"Bless you little birdies,
what kind of day is it?
Aren't you nice to visit me with song.
Is it warm enough on the other side?
I'll be coming out soon as I say my prayers,
soon as I find my shoes,
now don't you fly off without me—

three Hail Marys
and I'll be right along."

I wrote this poem when my mother was ninety-four and residing at an assisted living home in Maine. It was a lovely converted mansion on a hill with rolling lawns and a wrap-around porch. She'd sit out there all day in good weather, soaking in the light, the sounds of the trees moving in the wind, the birds. Three days before she died—a year ago August—at age ninety-nine, we sat on that porch singing every song she taught me as a child. Her fellow residents got a kick out of our version of "There Were Three Jolly Fishermen." My main goal in this piece was to capture her voice—to evoke her love for and sympathy with all living things. She really did talk to the world this way.

Dianalee Velie

METANOIA

*. . . To make injustice the only measure of
our attention is to praise the Devil.*
—Jack Gilbert

Talismanic rosary in hand,
I watch the breath of morning rise.
Warm mists, drifting upward
from the cold waters of the deep lake,
ascend into heaven. New clouds,
baby clouds form, from water to air,
a mystery unfolding before me.

Wafting east toward Mecca,
aglow with the rising sun,
they become angels with outstretched
wings, joining hands to worship the dawn.
Diminutive dots of dew descend upon
my cheeks, mix with a trace of tears,
uniting me with this celestial scene.

After all our sorrowful wailing,
are we not, after all, mostly water?
Infused with this infinite power
of transformation, my soul billows
with them; we are all one spirit
and permanence only a physical illusion.
The full moon still accents the shifting sky,

and day and night are one, until
a dove coos, cracking this scarlet code
of dawn. Then reality returns.
This simple reality: somewhere in a cell
your murderer still breathes, his breath
commingling in the atmosphere with ours,
until all our bodies eventually evaporate,

join as one. This unshakable reflection
acknowledges that these temporary
vessels we call home are merely swells
in an incalculably deep ocean,
so that even through tidal waves of griefs,
we must allow the longest night
to pull us back into the light,

risking forgiveness in our search for peace. . . .

—⊰

I wrote "Metanoia" to be the last poem in my book, *First Edition*. On September 6, 2002, my beautiful daughter-in-law, eight months pregnant with Jack, and my beloved grandson, Little Joe, were murdered in their Coconut Grove home, while my son was in Atlanta on business. This brutal murder devastated my son's life, my life, my daughter's life and the lives of Currie-Hill's family. Through the arduous and anguishing process that followed, our families eventually worked out a plea agreement, whereby the confessed murderer pleaded guilty. We spared his life by requesting that the prosecution drop the death penalty trial in lieu of this agreement, sparing us the horror of reliving those events through such a trial. The agreement was signed on March 17, 2005, nearly two-and-a-half years after the murders, with no trial date yet in site. *Metanoia* is a Greek word meaning "transformation." *First Edition* is a book about the journey through incalculable grief and "Metanoia" is the final poem about the transforming power of forgiveness.

Jeff Friedman

THE LONG HEAT WAVE

For Gerald Stern

Give me back the long heat wave, the sweat dripping
from eyelashes, the stained blouses, the black windows,
the spiders dangling from their silver bridges,
the wasps lighting on the branches of the cedar bushes
as they waited for me to make a dash for the screen door.
Give me back Herman Meltzer, our upstairs neighbor,
who forged his last check with a flourish before the police
took him away in his checked pajamas, handcuffed.
Give me back Hanna Gorelick in her red satin robe,
her hair in rollers; and Cathy Cowser naked in front of the window;
and "A Day in the Life" with its scratches and pops,
John Lennon singing "I read the news today, oh boy . . .";
and my thick brown hair—every morning
I brushed it down so hard my scalp stung, but the curls
sprung up before I left the bathroom mirror;
and my father warning the butcher at Sherman's Deli
not to trim off too much fat from the corned beef.
And give me back Barbie Silverman's long smooth legs
in her black short shorts, the Santa Maria rising from
the bottom of the river, the goddess undressing in the eye of the Arch
as the rabbis chanted to the brown muddy water.
Give me back the blue butterflies streaming
through the emptiness above the tall white sycamores,
the speckled blackbirds shitting on the Handshears'
new Oldsmobile, no matter where they parked.
Give me back my mother balancing her checkbook at the kitchen table—
"Everyone in Israel is beautiful," she says; and
my father in his shorts, thumbing through
a thumb-size version of The New Testament and
marking in red the passages he would use to make his sales pitch to the goyim,
raising his fist to the TV tube every time he hears
another special report—"But is it good for the Jews?"—
and my sister with her thick black hair,

waiting by the silent phone for a date to call.
Give me back the burning red coils in the sky, the plague of locusts,
God railing into the wind, the dark news that floats through the windows,
the spark of light at the beginning of our world.

I think the poem began when the poet Gerald Stern turned to me at breakfast one morning during a New England College MFA residency and said, "But is it good for the Jews?" I immediately broke into laughter because this reminded me of my mother and father, aunts and uncles and friends, all of whom would ask this question repeatedly after watching almost any news report on TV. I grew up in the fifties and sixties, and the memory of the Holocaust greatly affected our way of life and our identities as Jewish Americans. I started writing the poem with the refrain, "Give me back." The music drove the poem forward, connecting all the stories and images. Through the music, the world of the poem kept growing, taking in more stories, more history, more time and space. By the end of the poem, the speaker wants everything that has been lost back; it's a memorial to the world of our fathers and mothers, a lost world that had its beauty as well as its atrocity. The poem is about love and loss, which is the real subject of most poems.

Robert Dunn

GARNET

Embedded in the road cut

just north of highway 4

and you alone walking

                     may yet find

the frozen light of small red stars.

Walking by starlight

along a country road

you must remind

             your feet to stumble:

Finding the road (made for you alone)

adorned with semi-precious stones.

Of his showcase poem, Robert told a friend (paraphrased): "If you watch where you're going, you will never stumble into anything as wonderful as garnet embedded in New Hampshire granite."

Rick Agran

MUD REVOLVER

like a crow's vow to find
new mud to leave her footprints in
let's mint that print
onto all the world's moneys
onto all the thresholds of all the world's doors

who'd take the chance
to fly at all, even with *las angelitas negras*
if not for gravity's promised landings
bow-legged hop hop hop
skitter skip and stumble

soft green tussock of marsh grass for landing
quickly pluck the leopard frog
from his skin, turn his *chirrup*
inside out, leave him crying in his undershirt

no more eloquent than a handful
of mud wrapped in silver duck tape
some mud revolver, earthy thumbprint
at your temple, on the temple's stone step
two-legged hop of crow's touch-down

sparrow, little amnesiac, follows crow prints
through new snow, drawn like blue
to glacial ice or a raindrop to a dust cradle

by the Mad River's water-tangled weeds
grapevine and spruce bough, sparrow's lost
four-toed tracks disappear, her song's
a little heartbreak aria in blackberry bushes
then she remembers she can fly

A collage of inspirations, "Mud Revolver" was born on the banks of Campton's Mad River. In a riverside pine grove, a spring flood jumped the banks, filling the forest with jumbled slabs of turquoise-blue ice. In the branches above me, two crows, a lone bluejay, and a song sparrow flew concentric circles. A friend in Taos called that night. She spoke of crows as little black angels. I followed poet Robert Bly across New Hampshire for three readings. We share a love of darkness and mud, pregnant with metaphoric possibilities. His off-hand comment about economies created the idea of a common, crow-footed currency. Artist and naturalist David Carroll and I were discussing epigraphs. He'd joked, "No one ever quotes me . . ." so I "stole" an image from him: In a muddy swamp, he'd once come upon a shrieking frog skinned by a marsh hawk. His image offers the poem a sideways comment on the ineloquence of violence. A new war, coupled with the Patriot Act's zeal, worked to terrify young people I taught. They experienced forced complicity (in "blind following") as an anesthetic experience. The sparrow is their inventiveness; relieved of grief by her own song, she invents new possibilities.

Kathleen Fagley

WHEN I TURNED THE LINENS

A flutter of butterflies
flew out the window,
orange and black-winged,
the single blue and grey
silver-tipped quiver.
They had been in the bed all night
jewels resting in the dark warmth
between my thighs,
in my hair, curled
around my toe.
And then the morning light,
a few threads at a time through
filter of silky drapes
touched my forehead like grace,
lightening the pillow, the comforter
we threw off hours before.
I saw the blue brighten,
its slow creep through sheets and skin.
Huddled wings of butterflies
began their rustle,
brush of fur against mine,
imperceptible weight
like an air mail envelope
being opened slowly.
The message like mist,
then the falling steady rain
then its travel elsewhere.

"When I Turned the Linens," was one of those poems written spontaneously in a class following the principles of "Writing from the Heart," from a prompt: color photographs of butterflies and a bed. I took off with that image and voila—the poem in its entirely came to me. When people ask what the poem means, I don't know how to answer. The process was a mystery and I hope part of that remains for the reader.

Julia Older

BOOK BURNING

I was born fearless and fearless die.
You cannot kill the spirit of God in the name of God.
Forgiveness is the lifeblood of generations,
and it will take generations
to forgive what you are doing.

I am Fatima and Maryam
I am Muhammad and Christ.
I weep tears of blood
for the pitiful hatred
you have inflicted on this earth.

You could have made a fountain
clear as a mountain spring
but make a mire.
You could have built homes for the homeless
but build mansions of pleasure.

You could have given your flesh
to the luminous atoms
of peace and understanding
but give in to the intoxication
of warring and lust.

A poem learned by heart
cannot be burned.
When you are mortal as dust
on the desert of Dasht-e Kavir
I will still be here.

My *Tahirih Unveiled* sequence illuminates the life of poet Tahirih of Persia (ca. 1818–1854). A child prodigy (and bride), Tahirih prophesied the coming of the Prophet Bab. Although Babi (Baha'i) routinely were tortured and executed, Tahirih fled eight hundred miles across the desert to teach unveiled at Karbala and Baghdad. "Kill me if you like," she cried when captured, "but you can't stop the emancipation of women!"

Tahirih has carried me on quite a journey. For a collaboration project, fabric artist Rachel Lehr took my poem "First Veil" to her Afghan handwork collective and it returned exquisitely embroidered in silver and gold. Two years later the adventure came full circle when Rachel landed on my doorstep. "Hafiza asked to meet you," she said, introducing a dark-haired stranger, "and wondered if you'd show her the veil she embroidered." So here in my living room this Afghan sister recited by heart the poem she had embroidered during bombings in Kabul.

The final Tahirih poem, "Book Burning" was published in *Entelechy International* in 2003. That year Congress renewed the Patriot Act allowing Feds to confiscate library-book-user data—and America invaded Iraq. *Tahirih Unveiled* is dedicated to Iraqi diplomat Akila al-Hashimi (assassinated in 2003), Director Safia Ama Jan, Kandahar's Ministry of Women's Affairs (assassinated in 2006) and the struggle of all women who, veiled or unveiled, are silenced and invisible.

Sidney Hall Jr.

STRAWBERRIES

The strawberries are as
delicious as fire.

With milk and honey
they are like a lover,

mad, wild, foolish,
full of glee,

spotted, smooth,
sweet, a childish wine.

I bought them beside the road
from a Vietnamese farmer.

I tasted one and then
went back to his counter

and picked out two
more baskets.

He ducked
behind a wall

and quietly pulled
two extra of his best strawberries

and placed them on top
of my baskets

where I had to hold them on
with my thumbs.

→

I wrote the poem "Strawberries" when I was moving into a little cabin at Point Reyes in California, to write for a week. I had stopped at a highly recommended farm on the way there to buy some strawberries. A poem is never about what it is about—and is always about what it is about. Many of the poems I wrote that week were about fruit.

Cheryl Savageau

AMBER NECKLACE

inspired by ants
I tasted the sap
that oozed in great drops
from the bark of the pine
it tasted like its needles smelled
like winter like mountains or early morning
too strong for more than just a taste too sticky
to roll into the ball I wanted to carry in my hands like
a golden marble. I worried for the tree
was it hurt? I asked *no just leaking* my father told me
it's made so much extra food
he told me how even in deepest winter
you will not starve in a pine grove
how there is always food within
how the sweet globules turned over millions of years
hard as stone how the insects were caught inside preserved forever
it is not the insects I want but the sweetness they signify
I am caught in the sweet amber
of my mother's hair
nourished
by the light and dark of her
yes and the sticky
the too hard to manage
the I can't get it
off my hands
I want it now
those moments
of petrified love
where we first find ourselves
caught
before we know
what will preserve us

The poem "Amber Necklace" is one of a series of poems that were inspired by my mother's jewelry in the months after her death. I would hold a piece in my hands and a story or memory would come to me. These poems, in which I explore my mother's life and the mother/daughter relationship, became part of the book, *Mother/Land*.

This particular poem also bridges the different cultures of my mother (French) and my father (French and Abenaki). In western Abenaki tradition, human beings are made from trees, and in this poem, my mother literally becomes a tree, a part of the Abenaki land. The poem is in the form of a white pine on the page, which happened because doing the poem left-justified, as so many poems are, seemed too cold for the spirit of the poem. So I centered it, and it looked sort of like a tree. With a few tweaks, the pine tree became the final form.

Mark DeCarteret

PINK EYE

> *Objects on the beach, whether men or inanimate things, look not only*
> *exceedingly grotesque, but much larger and more wonderful than they really are.*
> —*Cape Cod*, Henry David Thoreau

What started out as a twitch,
the slightest pellet of distraction's
now the bust of a dignitary.
Two years I've housed this bladder
without mentioning God.
My mammoth boots sink into the sand.
A caretaker of some peculiar sabbath
I have only the steadiness of rain
to regulate my heartbeat.

The dunes are laden with shipwrecks.
Someone's slipper, more silverware.
A broken urn and these foot prints of black ash
leading out onto this staticky carapace.
How is it you'll be known to us now sweetness?

It's all I can do just to see through
the morning's new crust and its trickle of atonement.
Nonetheless, I don't appear as some ghost.
My muttonchops are busy with fleas
and my insides still host this revival.
Though I've detected a fresh sprite
operating in some faraway corridor,
many still refer to me as their home.
So I'll enlist yet more breakfast to combat the dream,
its awkward fin and the ocean's deafening premonitions.
Yes, lumps of gruel assuage most roars.

With century's end we turn to history,
see to restoring the soul's battered spine.
I cough up some fluid and reminisce.

Even with this little bit of sun I have difficulty gloating.
Here, where one world begins, and another has ended.
Though the water's glint is treasure to some
I acquire more grace merely blinking.
A moment to blot out the corpses
as they go about their business.

Boy, the episodes that provoked "Pink Eye" are a bit foggy, unlogged. An idea
arising as much from an advertisement for sties, this study for an experimental
treatment (poetry as protuberance, swelling, even somewhat of an affliction or
curse?), as Thoreau's excursions to the outer reaches of Massachusetts where he
was subjected to the wreckage of many a ship (as well as on Fire Island where
Emerson was "to charge" him in the retrieval of the remains of their friend Mar-
garet Fuller, a passenger on the sunken Elizabeth), thus poetry as recovery, sal-
vage, or in a remedial sense, potential cure-all or salve. And maybe some modest
and misguided version of what Harold Bloom refers to as a "shore-ode," verse
that "identifies night, death, the mother, and the sea." But basically I was struck
by this strange juxtaposition—the bereft hermit resigned to his calling, this mis-
sion, and those odd maladies, which not only impair or hamper the seeing of
anything through, but in some miraculous way, let it be recast, transfigured.

Catherine O'Brian

HISTORY

Somewhere the worm is turning.
My amah irons the white nightgown.
This is the only way to kill the tsetse fly's eggs.
My sister plays strip poker in the white nightgown.
My father bought it for me in Hong Kong.
He bought it from a crone.
The crone was carved of mammoth bone.
She was carrying a hundred white nightgowns on her back.
My grandmother tried to drown it in the well.
My mother stole it from under my pillow.
My mother gave it to the lavandera.
Pasing, the lavandera scrubbed it with
Fels-Naptha soap and bleach.
She scrubbed it so hard with a stone
It disappeared into the muddy Perfume River.

This poem was written during a time when I was obsessed with and possessed by one of my white nightgowns. I started to explore the image of a white nightgown—and wrote short poems on this subject for two years. The white nightgown became a symbol for me of imagination. When I slipped into my white nightgown, I was slipping into the world of my imagination and poetry. This poem was the first and opening poem in my manuscript. I thought the white nightgown should have a history. This history came out of a mix of my conscious and subconscious memories. This history includes my amah, who took care of me as a child, and the lavandera, who washed our clothes.

At the time I wrote this poem, my sister lived in Zambia, and she would write to me and tell me about the horrible flies which laid eggs under your skin, and how all clothes, even underwear, had to be ironed to get rid of them. My sister also loved white nightgowns.

Other images come from memories of growing up. In the Philippines and other Southeast Asian countries I would frequently see women, often very old women, carrying high stacks of clothing, cloth, food and wares on their backs. The faces of old women in the marketplace of Manila and Hong Kong were so strong, always vivid in my child's mind and imagination. I wondered about their lives . . . how hard their lives must have been.

My father often traveled throughout Southeast Asia. He would bring us gifts from his travels, small treats that would fit in his luggage; little carved elephants made of ivory. My grandmother was a little afraid of my writing poetry . . . and my mother loved the arts, but never really made art herself. Our amahs and the women servants usually wore white uniforms. Growing up I had often watched our lavandera and other women washing clothes—beating the laundry with a stone. The Perfume River was famous during the Vietnam War—it was known as a river filled with blood of many thousands of Vietnamese and American soldiers.

Joanne Merriam

FOOTPRINTS DRYING ON THE STAIRS

The sensations will germinate slowly. Too much can trigger rampant
growth, stems everywhere brown as footprints drying on the stairs and
with those insufficient thorns, but few flowers.

Better start them from the seed indoors, in baskets filled with peat
and woven out of all the ellipses and scraps of old verb tenses you
have lying around the house, watered by all you never say, weeks ahead
of their last frost date.

The buds will open crazy as bats in a crawlspace. But regardless,
after the blossoming, petals on the wind,

the going-to-seed. You want me to believe we aren't like those
flowers, your voice rough with the strain of all that watering.

Most of the poems for *The Glaze from Breaking* were written when I had just met
the man who is now my husband. I had seen a pretty awful late-night movie
about alien plants which grew so fast they could immobilize the hapless people
who found them, and that got me thinking. This prose poem was the result.

Neil English

SNEAK PREVIEW

We met six months
before your birth . . .
you stared out
in disbelief
with that "excuuuuse me" look
where your beautiful face
would grow to be,

sonogrammed so soon
into the present.

And I stared in
at the safety of your fetal nest,
hid my involuntary tear
from your mother's gaze
and prayed that,
in gestation time remaining,
we might make this world
a more peaceful place

for you

and all who follow.

Back in the summer of 2003, my daughter-in-law, Lisa, was expecting our first grandchild. I had stopped in for a quick visit on a Sunday afternoon. Lisa pulled an envelope from its perch on top of the refrigerator and excitedly asked if I'd like to see the images. I sensed exactly what was coming and said, "No thanks, I'm really into the magic and the mystery of birth and despite the technological advancements of sonograms, I need to wait it out, full term, just as I have patiently done for my own two children." I watched as her smile faded into disappointment, then utter bewilderment. Having thought it over, I apologized to Lisa for my archaic traditional position but she never offered the images a second time.

A couple of months later, I arrived in the morning at the house I was restoring in Deerfield and was greeted by the young woman at the door. "Would you like to see my new sonograms?" Sienna queried in a voice that took me instantly back to Lisa's only offer. Knowing, at that moment, that some hard-nosed traditions must evolve I said, "Yes, by all means, I'd love to see them!" The poem was fully developed by lunch break. As I jotted the first lines down on a scrap of spruce clapboard, I had no idea that the poem would shift into a prayer for world peace. That's the magic and mystery of the birth of a poem.

Lesle Lewis

THE CONTINENT BEHIND THE COLLEGE

A Soiree at the Sanitarium

A mother is killed on the highway, her fawn hovering over her body. By philosophy's time we're counted broke.

My cat is a rolling prime number on hot brick. The bricks wobble, convalesce, and hallucinate. The sanitarium has theme and piano, a tour about, and special beverage experiments.

We pray for the gift of longer life sentences. On the continent behind the college, many boys and girls lie resting.

The Dark Eye

We're good ninety percent of the time. We look work right in its dark eye.

The continent behind the college is spreading. It's not nonsense; it's Friday. An artist unhangs his show.

How the cracks between rocks and bricks fill with thyme, text and pots with sun, a television mutters, a mood shutters.

When you sit opposite from me at the café, I see what's behind you and you see what's behind me. Perhaps we should have been planning for this spontaneous conversation.

The New England Thinkers

Don't rush my sitting under the finch book tree. It has been dark for ten days and like two eyes feed one brain, we go driving. We are on an expedition to see the big numbers and wreckage of the floods.

We are in a clock shop.

→

The poem "The Continent Behind the College" was composed through a combining of journal notes over a period of several weeks and in particular notes taken while sitting in "retreat" on the patio behind the café at Landmark College where I teach. Some pieces of the poem come from the notion of any one spot in space and time having within it the wealth of a whole continent. In general, I'd say that a successful poem will surprise me and end up somewhere I never could have expected, in this case, a clock shop.

Christopher Locke

TELLING STORIES

When I was ten,
I said a crematorium
was an ice cream parlor
for dead people. Even as my father
laughed, I knew fire
ravaged the body, that it
shattered the hair first
and then peeled the clothes away.
But the invention felt good
on my tongue. All through school
I couldn't stop; hallways throbbed
with my voice, my deceit filling the air
with static and wonder: "The Spanish teacher
wants to sleep with me," I told friends
between the thin gray lockers; and,
"Thomas Edison almost married my great-grandmother."
My English teacher encouraged me
to write it all down;
my English teacher with a vein
of numbers tattooed on her forearm.
"We told stories to stay alive,"
she said. "To us, the Nazis
weren't even humans."
On the last day of school, our bus
stopped at a railroad crossing. My eyes
followed the boxcars as they lazied
by. I could picture the countless hands
sticking through the slats, rain skidding
across their fingers, their open palms
stunned by the chill of spring air.

I wrote "Telling Stories" as an homage to language. High school was one giant blind spot for me, but at least I did discover why storytelling, either through poetry, fiction, or face-to-face exchanges, mattered. And I owe the majority of this awakening to a handful of thoughtful teachers at Exeter High School who didn't necessarily "teach me" how to write, but who merely took their time to listen to me—something I didn't think adults were capable of at that point in my life. Ultimately, when I wrote "Telling Stories," my hope was I'd end up with a poem that believed in embracing those small moments that are true, even if it means eschewing the truth. Now, did I really see those boxcars? Answer that question with another: Would you believe the poem more if I did?

Pam Bernard

APRIL 1918

American Yankee Division training camp, near Rennes, France
(Excerpted from *Blood Garden: An Elegy for Raymond*)

> *Never such innocence again.*
> —Philip Larkin

i.

Rain has been continuous—
supply roads are muck beds full
of lorries sunk up to their axles, sodden
horses so weak from the crossing
they have forgotten their commands.
Drill fields are ankle-deep in mud.
At morning formations Raymond drops
from exhaustion and nearly drowns.

Tomorrow they leave finally for the front.

ii.

On the way, they are packed
into slatted cattle cars, others
on motor transports riding on
rubberless tires. Four months
in training with a wooden rifle,
now Raymond holds his brand new
Springfield on his lap.

For the first time he is frightened.
He can't remember why he is there.

iii.

The stench of the front finds Raymond
long before he arrives. Carbolic
and ether, human and animal parts
in sepsis and putrefaction, chloride of lime,

cordite, the sickly stink of gas.
And mixed with it all, the waste
of a million men. The smell reaches
back into the primitive realm of the brain.

Run, it says, and don't stop
until you are far away from here.

iv.

Young Raymond had spent the day
making land with his father. With wood
fulcrum and pry bar, they lifted
huge boulders onto the stone boat
hitched to the family's old black Percheron.
Her long hip and wide powerful thighs
made light work of their burden.

Almost nightfall—
Raymond commanded the last load
to meadow's edge, where a doe and her two young
fed—mute, indistinguishable from
what surrounded them—

The boy sensed movement and turned—
but by then they were gone.

This series of narratives about the Great War is from my book *Blood Garden*. My
father, who was well old enough to have been my grandfather, was one of the
first Americans to enter the First World War in the fall of 1917. When he landed
in France with his best friend from home, he was seventeen years old. Those
who survived the conflict were not encouraged to offer witness. In fact, the
opposite was almost always the case as boys returned to their lives with no way
to express their experience. Ghastly nightmares he called night horses were all
that surfaced of my father's life in the trenches, and he suffered them until the
day he died. While the truths of the war for many remain blurred by time, we
have other ways to remember—left as we are with a genetic memory that gets
passed down through generations, just as surely as abuse within a family. I wish
in these poems to address this consequence of the Great War, and, I hope, in
the process, all war.

Ralph Sneeden

COW'S NECK

"It isn't easy to turn your back on the past. It isn't something you can
decide to do just like that. It is something you have to arm yourself for . . ."
—V. S. Naipaul

With a bucksaw raised above his head
in surrender, he waded from my view
to where waves chewed the ankles of driftwood
mountains. He'd turn the stumps to lamp
bases, rip the planks to picture frames,
gifts for relatives, but most of it stayed
a dusty knot of bleached and broken trees
in our garage, something that could reach
and grab you if you were small, keep you from
the bike or shovel, the clam rake or net
you really needed.
                           In '65 I wouldn't
follow him to shore. Instead, I'd wait
in the bow, paralyzed, struggling to watch
him work between the intermittent backs
of lurching waves, sawing and dragging the limbs
to his pile. He set the tangled rafts afloat
then heaved them to the pitching rump of the boat
until I could barely see the white skull
of the engine cover beneath.
                                        This father,
the downed pilot, sprung from Baltic stalag
to wander a strange road home through many
kinds of freedom: the bodies bulldozed down
to common graves; the blanket-swaddled soldiers
staring from cold benches out to sea—
Atlantic City boardwalk rattling with traffic
of wheelchairs, the legless on crutches, the crazed
and shuffling whole.
                              Why did we return

each year to the horrible point of land
where the beach was choked by interlocked arms
of rotting pine and eroded oak? Why
use days of vacation to dismantle, import
that refuse to our home, hide it in rafters
or in the corner by a broken mower,
posthole digger, and the rest? His burned,
wet back and shoulders still whirl away
from me in foam and confusion, in water
mean as memory, cut, drifting, liberated.

"Cow's Neck" (1988) is an important poem for me because I wrote it at a time
when I lacked faith in my own experiences to drive narratives; it was safer and
more interesting to turn to the scanty images and fragments I had sifted from
what my father had told me about his experience in WWII, which had always
intrigued me. But the challenge of writing this poem was negotiating the con-
sciously evoked intersection of my father's story and my own. I was not only
determined to tap into what was mythic and monolithic to a war-free young
man writing in his late twenties, but to evoke—relevantly—the eerie and vio-
lent natural environment of that part of the South Fork of Long Island where I
had spent a lot of time as a child.

Until "Cow's Neck," I had done plenty of evoking, but with little insight or
substance, my attempts more like preliminary sketches for decorative water-
colors than poems. At that time, I had also been reading a lot of Dave Smith's
work, so some of the line-texture, syntax and diction certainly gained some con-
fidence from my being inspired by certain poems in *The Roundhouse Voices*. I am
heartened by the paradox of what happens when we mimic the poets we love,
finding our own voices by parroting others'. I also admired Smith's treatment of
setting (Tidewater, Virginia). It was his voice that carried me along. But I don't
write like this anymore. "Cow's Neck" first appeared in *The Sycamore Review* at
Purdue, in looser form. After finally deciding to include it in my book, I tried to
tidy and trim the lines into blank verse, hoping to coax out some subtle music
that was buried in the earlier draft, to give it a voice that would not seem too
blaringly out of tune with my other work.

Adelle Leiblein

CALLING TO THE SOUL OF MY UNBORN CHILD

I began it when the reign of our flesh
failed to bring us a child,
after years of my body emptying itself
over and over, the way the sky goes colorless
after the biggest storm of the year, a huge blank eye,
after I had learned how the needle swings, the dark bowel gurgles,
how the body sings a litany of curious cravings.
I began it when all my female parts clamped down
in sweat, and pleasure, and joy,
and no child came of it.

I began it when I had searched the face of my husband
who was searching mine for some slight shadow,
some mild betrayal, for some vague, soft holding-back.
I began it after I'd been warned by the roundness of pain,
been stuck with bleeding that goes unstaunched.
I began it when I had no other choice.

I take a book down off a shelf, I put it back again.
Waking from sleep I half-hear a fragment of my husband's mumble
as he drops off, ". . . love you,"
confirming in two words more than I deserve.
I do it when I'm alone in our house and say,
"When my child is my age it will be nineteen hundred and . . ."
knowing I must now rephrase.
I do it when I dream my lover a dowser,
and myself a silver strand just below the surface.
I do it when I wear black on black,
matching mode to mood, strong with power and resolve,
dark as the deepest soil, coal about to be diamond.

Once before lovemaking, I filled our room with lit candles,
laid out heaps of marigold petals and rice,
small plates of milk around the bed,
attar of roses on the pillows.

In the meantime, sweet husband asked,
"Would it help if I believed?"—an offering
in the face of all this daunting, amalgamated hope.
I couldn't bear to say *no* or *yes*.

I will do it knowing as I do
that wanting one man is dangerous, wondering
if wanting more than one is inevitable,
knowing that I am not the old dry wife,
but a sweet plowed acre . . .
I will do it because I know the discrepancy
between what we want and what we have.
I will do it in a hundred different guises,
more because of hope than of habit.

I will do it until I'm talked-out, wordless,
'til my child will hear me and move through that scrim
between this world and elsewhere,
until conditions of the universe are harmonious
and the child will come in me, and slip into her skin,
come in nakedness, breathing, rosy, and whole,
come to share with us this life on earth.

Calling to the Soul of My Unborn Child depicts a series of acts of self preservation. It voices my recognition that I'd taken on some almost ritualistic behaviors in trying to cope with my (our) inability to bring a child into the world. I think of the poem as an incantation or a spell, while others have called this poem a prayer. My intention in writing it was much the same . . . it was a cry of the heart. When I say it was a recognition, I mean that the actions of the poem, the calling, the yearning, were actual, and the pulling it all together in a whole single iteration was what brought it into cohesion, into its highest form—a poem— at least into the highest form I could make.

Ancient sages have said for millennia that our children pre-exist their birth, and that we must call them into this world. Another way of looking at it is the idea that we pick our parents. This can be a very scary thought for anyone who's ever been in therapy! This poem looks at it from the would-be parents' perspective, hoping to articulate the most sincere desire to welcome a child. Faced with a problem a poet writes a poem. Can I get an amen, somebody?

Hugh Hennedy

AGAIN IN THE GARDEN

Hanging from silver chains,
The fern and the fuchsia turn
To and away from each other
Like the gravest of dancers.
Leaves move in the breeze,
Willow and lilac and maple
And, beneath them, those
Of grass, while light and shade
Down there are mostly still.

Coming from some distance,
Traces of barking are,
If not golden, not
Brazen. The sun in the garden
Is warm and the voice of sparrows
Sweet as one brings seeds
To another and the fountain overflows again.

Some people might call where "Again in the Garden" got started a backyard
rather than a garden. I was, after all, sitting in back of the house on the lawn
under the old maple tree. And the fern and the fuchsia, the only plants in the
poem, are hanging from chains. But, I could reply, there were flowers bordering
the lawn, though they are not explicitly in the poem. And "the garden" is not,
finally, so much a place as it is a state of being, the state our parents are said to
have been in Eden for a while. It is that state that I set out to present when my
poem got started.

Maura MacNeil

THIS LAST PLACE

This change of light and how it wakes you with uneasiness
and the shift of wind from the north that rains down ice

might keep you covered for months. You swear this will
be your last season in a place you believe is disappearing.

These days everything keeps its place only for a moment
and then like magic it's gone. You don't trust the seasons

anymore. Your husband has moved the car to the other
side of the street to avoid a ticket without telling you

and you stand on the sidewalk looking at where it was parked
last night and doubt everything. You don't know how

you will remember anything anymore. You believe this change
happened quickly but you blink and remember that it did not.

In your dreams last night there were ships in the harbor run aground.
You think of changing your direction to find out if this is true.

The physical landscape that surrounds me, a landscape that has contributed
greatly to the creation of my internal landscape as a writer, has undergone rapid
change in the last few years. The lines "These days everything keeps its place
only for a moment / and then like magic it's gone" kept going through my head
as I drove through familiar space that became unrecognizable to me, overnight
it seemed, as new construction populated those landscapes. The poem began
as an attempt to reconcile this transformation and its connection to the unset-
tled shift I felt within myself as my sense of place, a place where my personal
mythology is so deeply rooted, is erased and replaced by the unrecognizable. As
the poem began to take form it moved into a broader context about how one
chooses to recognize their own self through the confusion and doubt that often
accompanies great change.

George Jack

BELOW THE ROMANTISHADOWS

Undercelebrated bit player,
Only love itself could give the tally of
How many sensual scenarios and
Seduction scenes in which you have played a
Supporting role, noncredited and
Conflagratiously standing aside, letting lovers
Occupy the spotlight, which ironically often
Only you were there to bestow upon them,
As they weave their impassionations into the realms and
Fabric of history, poetry, mythology
As you glow invitingly and observe politely,
Pyro-stemmed and posture perfect.

Promethiastically I observe the ritual, freshly
Releasing the sunset-silent slimcandesence of your
Wick-tethered kindle-symbol;
You are Venus De Milo's slowly receding right arm, your hand
Signs to me like a ballet-fingered arson-blossom.
I linger, rapt, as you relate to me in a kind of flicker-code
Details of the more legendary rendezvous
To which you were the essential, bystanderously immortal and
Interpersonal beacon of privacy.

Love is one of the oldest themes in poetry. One of the challenges of the writer
of a love poem is to make an attempt at exploring different perspectives of the
"love setting" as it relates to not just the sought after mood but the aesthetic
components of the piece; the impression of one lover through the other lover's
array of senses, the atmosphere in which a "love setting" takes place, both the
timelessness and the fleeting qualities of the love ideal's logical extension.

"Romantishadows" is a perspective on not one particular "love setting," but
a celebration of a particular stereotypical element in the "love scene." Since
the light and heat given off by a candle flame seems to be dispensed up and

out with a certain frugality of temperature and energy, I attempted to make sure that the descriptive terms utilized had a calm economy to them as well. For example, "Conflagratiously" is intended to convey both a depiction of the flame and temper—that with an idea, there is a graciousness with which it burns and dispenses the gift of its power. Ironically, the object that the speaker looks toward to "emblemify" love may never truly know love because it may only participate in the action of love as actor in the background; this piece is my attempt at venerating all love scenes from arguably one of love poetry's more venerable vantage points.

Robert W. Crawford

THE EMPTY CHAIR

Out on the rocky point there stands a white
And isolated Adirondack chair.
The tourists take a snapshot of the sight—
But only if nobody's sitting there.

I guess they know, without fine arts degrees,
The standard first-term lesson, "less is more."
It's all about the possibilities
And the importance of the metaphor.

The focus isn't on the lovely ring
Of blue in which the empty chair is framed—
Where ocean meets the sky—it's on the thing
That in an artful picture can't be named:

They save a central place for what might be—
A certain absence, looking out to sea.

While staying at The Driftwood Inn on Bailey's Island, Maine, I noticed that guests were drawn to take photos of a white Adirondack chair that was placed on a rocky point overlooking the Atlantic, but they would always insist on taking the pictures while the chair was empty—no Uncle Alfred ruining the artistic shot!

When I got back home, during a poetry tutorial, I used this observation to make a point about the importance of leaving room for the reader in a poem—how an Uncle Alfred, in all his specificity, really would wreck the composition. We were outside on a beautiful August afternoon and I remember becoming quite animated about the whole thing. It was there that the poem came into existence, though it wasn't until two months later that the "certain absence" was added to the last line actually finishing the sonnet.

Maren C. Tirabassi

SACRED SPACE

Buddha under the
cross,
rice grains, lotus, incense
balanced on a rack of hymnals.

The funeral is prepared
in the congregational church
for the man who taught
tai chi,
and his students do their forms
in the aisles, the chancel,

quiet, graceful,
round movements,
gathering
air
with the arms of their loss.

Speaking for God,
Isaiah said—
my house shall be a house
of prayer
for all people.

Jesus of Nazareth and
Siddhartha Gautama,
agreed.

Psalm or mantra—
the wind of all our turning.

→

This poem is a tribute to the hospitality of the good folks at Northwood Congregational Church, UCC, who welcomed a funeral for a local Buddhist during the Christian sacred season of Lent. There was no moment of hesitation at the sanctuary alterations that greeted and comforted those who grieved. One of the most important things to me as poet and pastor is to open doors to all the possibilities for human experience of the Divine. I was able to tuck Judaism, Christianity and Buddhism into these lines and would have included Muslim, Shinto, Baha'i, and Hindu thought, but that would have turned the poem into a tract!

Maggie Dietz

MATTHEW 6: 19–21

Hold off awhile, moth and
rust and thieves—for I love

this world, my heart is
here, where a body breathes.

I've seen such treasures, even
of your making: night's wool,

the frayed holes light comes
through. Burnt sky cracking

the corroded ocean Octobers
the sun goes. Thieves have

taken grief, and the thing
one hated most. So keep

your work up elsewhere, leave
me my store. The young

geologist radioed THIS IS
IT before St. Helens sank

him, seized in his dream:
treasure of rupture and force.

What does one fear if not a
loss? How do days in the next

world pass? Nothing to tend,
nothing you're up against.

No moth, no rust. O Lord let
there be thieves among the angels.

The verses the title refers to, in the King James Version, are: "Lay not up for yourselves treasures upon earth, where moth and rust doth corrupt and where thieves break through and steal: But lay up for yourselves treasures in heaven, where neither moth nor rust doth corrupt, and where thieves do not break through nor steal: For where your treasure is, there will your heart be also."

The poem was missing some element until I read a story in the *New York Times* on the anniversary of the 1980 Mt. Saint Helen's eruption, in which the geologist David Johnston (and many others) perished. It was Johnston's last words that struck me with a kind of happy pain—how thrilled and moved he seemed by the great geological occurrence (a kind of natural masterpiece) that would take his life; somehow the words, his experience, got at the heart of the question of where one's treasure is, how fiercely we cling to our terrestrial gifts and loves.

Elizabeth Knies

THE SLANTED BIRCH

Happiness is hard to put words to.

From my window I see
a small bit of woods

where tan leaves pool
around the feet of trees.

Across the verticals
of charcoal and brown

a white birch slants—
brilliant against the neutral plane.

The poem "The Slanted Birch" was written shortly after I moved from Kingston to Portsmouth in September of 2006. I'd had several rough years following the death of my husband in early 2002, and being back in town felt like a fresh start. I took quiet pleasure in looking out of the windows of my apartment at the neutral tones of trees enlivened by a slash of brilliant white.

Andrew C. Periale

CAT AT SUNDOWN

No doubt about it: the cat's a pill—
sharpens claws on table legs,
refuses to be pampered,
yowls incessantly—
and one that's really hard to swallow.

But now the cat's gone hollow.
Hard to say what's different—
he still perches on his pillow
yet his eyes no longer follow me
across the room. Mice come and go
without disturbing Kitty's catatonia.
This beast I lately loathed
I now bear to and from his litter box,
fuss over each successful bowel movement.

Last month, he wouldn't let me touch him,
now he suffers these indignities without complaint.
That's how it goes with families:
One has notched another's ear,
pissed in an inconvenient place
or knocked a treasured heirloom to oblivion.
In the end, the only thing that matters
is to be there,
stroke the soft, warm fur
and wait for night to come.

I lead a number of creative writing classes at area high schools, and sometimes I scribble along with my young artists, particularly during those quick "kick off" exercises at the beginning of class. Working from the purloined prompt (pick-pocketed from a Portsmouth poet) to write about a cat (not your own) who has nothing to live for, I penned this gem with the sense of surprise my cat displays at the appearance of an extremely large fur ball.

Bill Garvey

TAMPONS

In our town's Post Office
I read the letter from Iraq
next to Wanted Persons—
from a Sergeant Robert Diaz
whose list of needs
includes toothpaste, Crest,
he specified, and
toilet paper, any brand,
wet wipes, Snickers bars,
Mach 3 razor blades—the best,
Kleenex, Dial soap, bubble gum . . .
I stop, squint like a child who
thinks he found the word
that doesn't fit the rest.
As if to explain, Diaz
wrote, *to plug bullet holes.*

The genesis of the poem, "Tampons," came from an actual letter my wife and I read in a small Vermont town. We got there early to see a play at the community center, bought sandwiches and Cokes at the general store and killed time. A post office in back of the store posted a letter from a soldier in Iraq, next to Wanted Persons. He asked for things we take for granted that make life a bit more comfortable. I read the letter thinking of this kid from Vermont, stationed in some hell hole, hungry for a Snickers bar. When I got to the last item on his list, tampons, and his explanation, the war came home to that little store. I wonder to this day if the soldier worded his letter with intention, to bring the war home as we drink Cokes and move through life as if Iraq were on another planet. Whatever his intention, I will never forget his letter.

Scott Coykendall

BLIND
For Jeff

There is so little difference between absolute dark and pure light. Once,
my parents pulled over beside a Missouri highway to tire the kids out
with a four dollar tour of a show cave. The bored teenaged guide
    slumped
from plaque to plaque, reciting the script as if it were the white pages
from some distant city. "When I touch this switch," he warned in the
    deepest intestine
of the cave. "You will be in darkness more complete than anything
    you've ever known."
He fixed his eyes over our heads. "Darker than space," he added, as if
    we weren't
frightened and confused enough. Then, for an instant, he introduced
    us to an absolute.
Light had never been. Cornfields had never happened. My Motley
    Crue tee shirt
was a dream. I might have panicked had it not been for the sound of
    our guide
counting twenty to himself.

We circled the sun some more, and it happened again: another road
    trip. Rain
hammering earth. While I rode shotgun, Jeff drove my car and
    smoked
and held forth on the Navy, Melville, the Kansas City Chiefs, and sex
    magic.
He was still explaining the latter when lightning shattered the world.
    White lines and black road
disappeared. Our hands, our faces, our cigarettes, our dashboard
    vanished. Thunder
jumped us and ran. For an instant, we might have heard our tires
    rolling
on wet pavement. Rain. But mostly we heard me: "The car is fried!
    The car is fried!

Hit the brakes! Everything's fried!" I wailed. "Cool your shit," Jeff
    growled, and grabbed me
with the hand that was neither driving nor smoking. "We're blind right
    now."

This last time? The world gray with ash and concrete. Day meaning
    night. Flesh meaning
nothing. Suddenly, there were people in the air. All night, we saw
    people in the air. Everywhere
we looked. I kept picking up the phone, with the hand that was not
    holding my children.
I called my parents. I called Jeff. I asked everyone I love, "If we wait a
    minute, will we see again?"

A mutual friend, John Gilgun, emailed me a few years ago and asked me to write
a birthday poem for our friend Jeff's fortieth birthday. Jeff and I had had a lot of
great times, but I don't do occasional poems very well. I sat to write down about
a road trip and lightning strike that we had been involved in. It was one of our
favorite stories. But the war in Iraq was starting, the television was still showing
the twin towers falling every night, and I was having a hard time excluding the
world around me from my poem about this comic moment. And, in truth, Jeff
was one the first people I called the night of 9/11. Finally, I surrendered and let
the world into the poem. No one has asked me to write a birthday poem since.

Lisa Bourbeau

CADENZA
For Adeline Brown

it's a trap, addy
this life, or the next

fog under fingernails,
sea glass fragmenting the sill,
the sleight of hand of rivers, dark woods,
shallows deepened churning shadows,

. . . a constant
shucking off of light . . .

weeping cherry, dragonfly, dwarf iris, phlox . . . .
and the early shoots!
they are green enough
for one whole shrunken season.

each matters
or not
first and last

to stand against and be defined by

this sky
that inclines itself toward
nothing—

. . . to be sheer color,
cloud burdened, without shape,
estranged . . .

see the moon, held captive
in each pale curl
of breath. always
the eye persists, steel jawed,
snapping away

fallen

crumbs in an apron pocket
a nest under the eaves
twilight reshaping
the harsh lines

impeccable distance

cruel as barbed wire strung
against an otherwise kind
but wholly imperfect
white expanse

The poem "Cadenza" was written for, and to memorialize, Adeline Brown, an extraordinary woman and a beloved friend. Addy fiercely fought and last year lost her battle with ovarian cancer.

Katherine Solomon

NEAR FIRENZE

If I had not been standing on that ladder with the sun
just so on the weathered wall . . . if I had not
been reaching to retrieve the hair clip
that had slipped from my fingers a moment before
as I leaned from an upstairs window
        into this very postcard
of a morning . . . and if
that barrette had not been caught
by the rosy ledge below . . . and if you
        had not called out my name
from the shade of that shed, raised your hand
to show me where you stood—only your hand visible
as it moved into stunning brightness . . . and if I
had not clutched the jutting brick for balance
as I turned,
        so that when I turned back
to face the wall again, my eyes held the image of two
hands: yours, fading as I blinked, above my own . . .

I might never have seen those four faint crescents
in the clay: those marks like a few days
from a calendar of lunar modes,
        those fingerprints
left by someone with bigger hands than mine,
someone long ago who must have been the one
to smooth the mortar when the suncooked wall was new.

He must have reached for balance too, and left his mark
between the bricks, grasped the sill as I did
when someone called to him.
        Or was it the perfume
of a woman's hair as she passed below that turned
his head? Was he startled by an unexpected sound—
not a loud one: the prints aren't deep enough—

a single strand of music,
some half-heard song that brushed his cheek,
tickled his ear, in its rush down the long colonnade
of time and sunlight?

When I received a postcard from friends visiting Tuscany, I propped it against my computer as a focus for daydreaming. The postcard showed a farmhouse, the kind that has often been turned into a vacation rental under the agritourism movement. A shed and a ladder were faintly visible at one side.

I'd always wanted to go to Tuscany, and found I was inserting myself into the postcard when I looked at it, standing outside below a second story window at first. Before long, in my imaginings, I was inside the second story room, looking out at the landscape from that window, my hair still long and blonde, held back with a hairclip. I never meant to write a poem, but I began to imagine one, a what-if poem: what if I really had been there, what if I dropped my hairclip, what if I climbed the ladder? The rest is . . . well, more imagining. The poem developed as part of my daydreaming, and as I began to "hear" it, I gave myself an exercise: to extend the what-if's until I found the story.

Matt W. Miller

BALLISTICS

That the greasy pop-pop
of a semiautomatic wrecks

the air before I can get off
the couch, before my wife yanks

our baby daughter
from the new fallen flesh

of pomegranate and runs
inside before their car horrors

past our fence is true.
That this winter this town

has more bullets than rain
gutters in truth but is not true. But the bullets

are true. Candles, rosaries, the roses
that shrine the street corner

are true beyond the next-day stare
of faces watching me walk

behind a stroller. What's true
is the wound

channel, that human tissue jumps
from a bullet like water

from a diver. One
boy bled out where he fell

The other on a table
at a university hospital. Drawn

blinds are true, checked locks. Smiles
have too much teeth to be true.

What's vital is the crush
mechanism, the permanent hole

a bullet makes in that moment
I'm watching

my wife and child each time
they fail to reach

the door. Noises at night grow
skin, grow fur, spring fangs

that scratch and score casement
glass and hinge

between what's true. And what isn't?
That I wrote down the names

of the dead, though it should be.
What's real are the costs

of moving, of staying, the recoil
from a too early doorbell,

the ten to fifteen seconds left
to a body when the heart's

instantly destroyed. What's left
is our fence five feet from

the street, the house thirty feet
from the fence, the front wall

four inches of California
bungalow and then her crib.

I was living in East Palo Alto, a rough neighborhood a couple miles from Stanford University. One Sunday afternoon as my wife and baby daughter were playing outside of the house we were renting, two kids were gunned down just around the corner. The assailants sped past the yard as my wife pulled our daughter inside. For a while I was just numb with shock and fear for my family. For some reason, I started reading FBI reports on what bullets do to the body. In doing that I found the poem and a way to process the experience.

Liz Ahl

SETTING TYPE

One at a time, I slide each character upside down,
into the composing stick, cool steel in the palm of my hand.

Drawn from the shallow, divided drawer, each letter
is a step towards a word, each word slowly progressing

toward meaning. The afternoon light is so late,
every still thing casts a dramatic shadow—

even the blocks of type, already set, elongate,
the cast edges of the letters lengthening across the table.

This work stretches even longer than the shadows,
and by the time I hit a rhythm, a fairly steady click

of letters into place, I'm no longer tethered to language.
I'm an assembly line, and I'm building this thing

I can't see yet, a page of text polished up and finished
in a future so distant it seems foolish to think of it.

My fingertips and thumbs are smudged with meaning.
I'm not looking for the story, but feeling instead

the sheer heft of sentences—lead characters bound
into blocks and tied with string, the literal weight of them

in the galley tray, the thing they say to my fingers,
my forearms, the pits of my elbows,

the immediacy of an ache creeping through my shoulders
as I tie off one last block.

→

Whenever I work on a typesetting project, I'm struck by how language seems to disassemble, even as I'm literally assembling words. Type is heavy and dirty and tiny, and building a stanza of text becomes this purely physical act. This act, in turn, reminds me (why do I always forget?) about language as a physical thing. Words have weight. Even empty space (leading, made of strips of—you guessed it—lead!) has weight and must be accounted for.

I have also occasionally done minor edits on poems as I was typesetting them—I think this is a result of the combination of the slow pace of the work and the physical wrangling of lines. In recalling the work of this poem, I remember deciding that the couplets did a decent job of giving this poem a good amount of white space, slowing its pace a bit. There's a lot of starting and stopping in setting type. I hope this poem describes for readers both the physical and metaphysical experience of this kind of work.

Kate Gleason

TERMINATION SHOCK

From my mother's hospital window at dusk

The horizon is all pines, ragged as the deckled edge of paper
as if the sky were being torn from the earth. Inside,

a line has been started, the IV drip a water clock of salt
ticking its slow solution into her, not into her arm

but into a port they've implanted in her chest
to spare her the needle-sticks' cumulative pain, so much

will be taken from her, so much given. Three rounds
of chemo have leveled her leukocytes, her white cells

unresponsive, her count down. She needs her rest,
her eyes closed but not yet following the swift

volley of dreams. I open a worn issue of *Time*
where the space probe Voyager is on the last leg of its journey

out of our planetary system into empty space.
It's beginning to cross the place called the *termination shock*

where the incoming wind formed by the death-bangs of stars
makes the solar wind stop expanding by pressing from without.

It's the type of thing I would read to her, but she has dropped off
to sleep, her chest rising and falling, the gentlest of seas,

as if the blast-cells in her blood weren't starving her of oxygen.
Outside, the blue blackens, the dark drifts down, the window

becoming a mirror the night holds to my breath,
my face weary, its lines deeper. Above me, the balloons

from yesterday's visit already begin to wither,
tapping at the dotted tiles of the lowered ceiling.

→

This poem began when I was sitting in my mother's hospital room as she lay dying. I was reading an article in *Time* magazine about NASA's Voyager space probe, which was then passing through an outlying region called "the termination shock" on its way out of our solar system. Nearly thirty years earlier I had watched Voyager's launch. I had been fascinated by the fact that the probe carried a golden gramophone record (a sort of prototype of the compact disk) containing samples of sounds and images meant to represent who we were as Earthlings to any space travelers who came in contact with the probe. Three decades later, there was something resonant about this little compressed time capsule of humanity leaving our system while my mother was passing through the darkness at the end of her life. Many drafts later, I arrived at "Termination Shock."

Don Kimball

DEER IN A CRAFT SHOP

It might have been the early morning light
that caught her eye, while she dashed down a one-
way street that night, persuading her to cross
a wide divide—where, later in the day,
she would've had to wobble in the sun
for speeding cars to stop, before she'd dare
to trot the crosswalk. Now, beguiled by some
random need, she strides the four-lane street,
smashing through glitter into shards of glass,
and leaping down, not onto moss or leaves,
but the astonished sales floor. Mouths agape,
the city road crew stand outside to watch,
while the whitetail doe negotiates
a labyrinth of narrow aisles. "Oh, no—
there goes another vase!" yells one of them.
She stops behind a shiny case, as if
gazing with longing at a silver bracelet,
appraising the delicacy of her plight,
when light, that winking light, bewilders her,
invites her back to thrash some inner darkness,
where she attempts to vault a jeweler's bench
and leaps, with a shatter of window panes,
into the blinding glare—a wounded doe
falling two stories to a parking lot,
hobbling a trail of blood and broken vases.

My poems are often sparked by an anecdote, something I've read, a dream or
what I've been privileged to observe. This poem began with an event I read about
in our local newspaper—which bothered me for days until I wrote about it.

Midge Goldberg

WALKING ON ICE

Foot traffic on the lake's increasing lately.
The fishermen are out without a boat,
Building fires and drilling holes sedately
In the only thing that's keeping them afloat.

Some folks are skating, measurers who know
The thickness of the thing, the hard and soft
Of it. They don't mistake the ice and snow
For something magic keeping them aloft.

The only ones unsure out here are geese,
Who clamor cautiously onto the lake.
The fact that they can fly gives them no peace—
Their wing-and-prayer approach to what might break

Recalls what lies beneath, how footing changes,
How pressure builds and cracks and rearranges.

Having grown up in Florida, I have never become comfortable with stepping out onto a frozen lake up here in New Hampshire. No matter how thick people tell me the ice is, no matter if I see giant pickup trucks driving out onto a lake, I still always have this irrational fear that the ice will break right where I am, and I will fall through and be trapped beneath. Every year I conquer my fear and walk out on the lake by my house for the thrill of looking back to the beach where we swim each summer, and it seems a sort of magic to me. But I'm always amazed at how no one else around me seems to notice that we could perish at any moment!

One year, watching some fisherman blithely go out on the lake, and then seeing some geese be as tentative as I was, got me thinking about possible metaphors of the frozen lake and how we think about it.

Patrice Pinette

HERE

do you know nothingness
                     this is where I find it
         among miles of heather
                     purple red orange burnt orange
    stretching over the highlands in Scotland
                and there in the peace of no bird
             no rustling thing no silent deer all alone
               I ask God to speak to me
and in the silence
             what does He say
                        nothing
nothing

do you know nothingness
            that is the most powerful
      absence
          the miles of heather all around no bird no
    sound even the silent deer are nowhere
               and I say God can you speak to me
       then of course I listen with might
                 and expectation empties

when no other voice says

I am here

→

The poem "Here" arose from someone else's story. Although I had been to Scotland, it was hearing another speak of the profound silence and stillness there in the stark and beautiful Highlands that prompted not only a memory, but an awareness of a corresponding inner landscape—equally still, and always present.

Jane Eklund

CREDIT IS A FICKLE MISTRESS

When I open my credit card bill I have to sigh a little
for the models in the catalogs, the ones who gaze back at me
with their come-hither looks, the ones who assure me
that I would be beautiful, if only I were already
beautiful and wore fashionable clothes.

While I make out the check, I imagine handing it directly
to the blonde who pouts out from page 31,
which is conveniently located on the coast of Nova Scotia,
a place I've never visited but am well outfitted for.
She takes the money, tucks it in the pocket

of her pleated-front poplins, in classic navy,
$38.50, then goes back to staring coolly at the Bay
of Fundy. She's clearly not interested in me
or the stack of bills waiting like a suitor
on a kitchen table in New Hampshire, where it's still winter

and the ocean does not beckon like a promise or even
a lie. It's true I'm in over my head, I can't even think
of anything to say to this woman who wants nothing
but my platinum MasterCard as compensation
for my few salacious thoughts, so long as they don't interfere

with her walk on the beach in the interest of capitalism
and tasteful sportswear. Besides, she's too young, too tall,
has a boyfriend waiting in a tan corduroy blazer
by the lake on page 60. Credit is a fickle mistress:
It's the price you pay for shopping by charge,

for wanting what you can't afford, for getting a season
ahead of yourself. By the time I've finished emptying
my bank account into separate envelopes, she's already
on another beach, in Nantucket, this time in an ecru
bathing suit with scooped back and scalloped neckline,

glancing petulantly toward the sea-green sea, under the blaze
of the burnt-umber sun, and—oh—the cerulean sky . . .

→

With the decline of the art of letter writing, the mailbox at the end of my drive-way is typically filled with two things these days: bills and catalogs. One day I set about imagining my way out of the former and into the latter.

Ardelle D. Osborne

LOVE STORY FOR THE LITTLE YELLOW FISHES

We want to eat fishes
but there are no fish.
Each clumsy boat
resting buoyant as balloons
on the Ionian Sea gives
us the same answer—no fish.
Eventually in an ocean-side
taverna he buys
seven fresh spiky yellow
fish and takes them in
a plastic bag to the stony beach.
For half an hour he squats
where water touches his feet
and, with a delicate knife, scores
each, feeling the depth
to the backbone. With his huge
thumbs, he rolls
back the flesh, probing
the pink billows. He eviscerates
them, throwing the entrails
to the gulls swirling like
kites above. Concentrated,
he never looks at me. He
tenderly washes their gutted
bodies in a green plastic
pan with seawater, places
them back in the plastic
bag, then looks up and smiles.
Later, on the little stove
in the room, he simmers
them, graced with oil
and lemon, bony but delicious.

It is strange to be on a Greek Island surrounded by a sea of fishing boats and not be able to find fish to eat. Actually it's downright frustrating, and why there was a problem I never did find out. My Greek poems are full of fish and water, but on this island and at this time of year (just before the tourists arrived) any decent food was difficult to find. There was one restaurant which served only beef, and this in itself was an oddity because as good as the meat might be to begin with it always ended up ruined! The island was beautiful however, and out of season we felt pretty exclusive.

Hope Jordan

MERRIMACK

River pushes up
sky sinks down

Slow, the drift
the buoyant sprawl

Root, mud and rock
the current shifts

An early star
gleams in the treeline

Peace, the cliff swallows
speak with their wings.

I moved to New Hampshire twenty years ago and have been in love with it ever since. I'm lucky enough to live within a short walk to the Merrimack River; that's where I go when I need to decompress. I write a lot about the land here and I used to write a lot of free verse; it wasn't until about five years ago at a conference that I became reacquainted with writing in form. I try to let the poem tell me what kind of form it wants to be in. This poem came from an exercise I did for a graduate level poetry class at Plymouth State University with Liz Ahl.

James Rioux

GENRE

Novels abandoned . . . The physical strain
of characters living in muscles, plots
tangled in nerves behind the eyes for months,
whole years perhaps sleepless, waking dreams
smothering what each day may hold. And so
only chapters, paragraphs, sentences, words
bound in sound-clusters, rhythm worn smooth
from rubbing, words become lives themselves, lives
not much like our own but recognizable—
endings far too often violent, abrupt.
And though they suffer our bodies but briefly,
many take to healing and miracles.
For them, there is no marriage, no home.
They raise no children. They raise the dead.

"Genre" was born, like most poems, out of tension. In this case, I was struggling
with some unfinished writing projects and my body needed these words to artic-
ulate a set of complex feelings concerning language and personal motivation.

Poems featured in

W. E. Butts's Poet Showcase

(2009–2013)

Patricia B. Fargnoli

ON THE QUESTION OF THE SOUL

It is not iron, nor does it have anything to do
with the fleshy heart. It does not quiver
like feathers, nor the arrow shot from the hunter's bow,
is not the deer that runs or falls in the snow.
It hunkers down in the invisible recesses
of the body—its closets, scrolled bureaus,
the ivory hardness of the chest,
or disperses through every cell. And also it flies
out beyond the body.
Someday watch smoke travel through the air.
Someday watch a stain spread out to no stain
in the ocean. The soul does that.
It doesn't care whether or not you believe in it.
It is unassailable and contradictory: the dog
that comes barking and wagging its tail.
It is not, I am certain, biology.
Not a cardinal or a heron, not even a thrush or wren,
but it might be a praying mantis.
It is the no color of rain
as it sweeps a field on an August morning
full of fences and wildflowers.
It is the shifting of light across the surface
of any lake, the shadows that move like muskrats
across a mountain whose shape mimics the clouds above it.
Weighed down by the vested interests
of the body it, nevertheless, bears us forward.

For many years, in the poetry world, there has been an unwritten rule that certain words aren't acceptable in contemporary poems either because they have become clichés or because they are too "poetic" or "sentimental." Until recently, one of those words was "soul." What I was taught was: you can't use the word "soul" without defining it. In this poem, I'm attempting to do just that.

James Duffy

DO NOT MISS WHAT IS HERE

The machine under the skin
makes up the logic now and then
a land of stone and cold wind.

It is difficult to see a hair
at midnight. These windows
are absurd. What can I sketch on the walls?

Wild West. White City. Electricity
Building. I wave sadly
at the butterflies, catacombs of

beetles, some leaves on the tree
that remain. A small red glow that
moves abruptly. Sweet grass

folds in presence. I hear an owl call.
Fools Crow could travel for days outside
his body when he spit on the lodge stones

igniting his prayer.
Thomas Edison said man is a
systematically managed

corporate machine whose units—endowed
with great intelligence—concentrate
in small cells like towns

within which many citizens dwell.
Mullen seeds—dormant for
hundreds of years—are known to sprout

hold and heal scarred earth.

Something is happening meanwhile.
The light grows out again the disarray
of sunrise. I distinguish more certain shapes.

→

"Do Not Miss What is Here" reflects my ongoing concern with our ecology. I am also ever aware—when I attempt to write poems—of the gap between language and experience and how one seeks to make order out of seemingly random thoughts and events in search of meaning, freedom, love, control, and security. Fools Crow was a Native American healer who helped negotiate an end to the standoff at Wounded Knee.

Alexandria Peary

THE EGYPTIAN TOMB OF EMILY DICKINSON

The author reading in her grave is an orange dotted line
then a red continuous line, a house light & more head lights,
above that, a row of (etc.), what a car alarm looks like:
4 signs repeated together: a cherry, a pineapple, cloud, raindrop &
then brief yellow dashes moving like birds, "To be continued."
The red line lies above the orange line at 75 mph
on the mountains on the last page—while a crow goes
from behind, deleting the orange dotted line—each dash
worth 5 points, cherry and pineapple 10 points, the glow-in-the-dark
haystacks & speeding garbage truck, 50—through
to the underlined parts of the room where I write.
The red line lies above the orange line at 75 mph
on the mountains on the last page in the dark morning.
She reads and reads in this large building in a room
in western Massachusetts—in this primitive dark
a fish skeleton goes by. The walls are decorated with
repetitions, electronic and natural sounds, someone coughing,
an alarm clock going off. A large gloomy ballroom
with an answering machine, & then a black mental swimming pool
ended by three dots.

This poem was a breakthrough for me, written when I lived in Northampton, Massachusetts, a few miles away from the home and literal grave of Emily Dickinson. I tried to structure the poem like the music of Philip Glass, specifically, using the way his repetitions evoke strips of color. Of course, it is also one more homage to the most beloved of poets. I wanted to give her another grave, one with an open door. I wanted to give her a final home different than the one physically located in Amherst, with its stone decorated with drippings of candle wax and dried petals left by fans. Overall, my poems are meta, or interested in drawing attention to the presence of language—such as is the case with this poem. Meta writing, I suppose, is another way to also bring mindfulness into the act of writing and reading.

Martha Andrews Donovan

HER STORY

They were wild trips, those journeys
up the narrow ghats that wrapped around
the mountains of my mother's youth.

The buses had no windows, no sides,
only poles from which my mother swung,
this child with a passion for the sudden.

Her missionary mother was sure
she would be flung down the steep side
of the mountain, lost to the wildness below.

What did my mother care of that?
She was a child, full of audacity;
she loved to hear herself shriek.

And now, tethered to her dying
bones, what would my mother give
for the sureness of her youth?

So let her drape her washcloth on her head
for a crown. Let her fling herself outward,
head first. Oh God, let her shrieks fill the room.

"Her Story" is the first poem in *Dress Her in Silk*, a collection of poems that places my mother's dying of cancer in the context of her unusual childhood in rural South India as the daughter of missionaries. In this poem, I recall the stories my mother told me of the wild journeys from the plains of Podili up the Western Ghats to Kodai where she attended boarding school. As poet, I try to capture the audacity of youth that struggles to persist, even in the face of great suffering.

Grace Mattern

CIRCLING

You could keep up with me and even better me
in some competitions, my basic criterion,
someone fast at my side and now there's no
companion so I move faster than ever,
I talk as I walk between meetings, mini-meetings
while moving room to room, up and down
stairs, I walk as I talk to friends, circling
the table, alone, carrying my nugget of darkness,
my nugget of gold, moving back and forth
across the line so often the line has rubbed out.
I hold the edge and let people look over
my shoulder to see what is there, what is not.

"Circling" is a poem from the book *The Truth About Death*, which chronicles the year after losing my husband to ocular melanoma. The poem documents a shift in my year of grieving, when I began to get glimpses of how to carry the loss of my beloved life partner as a strength, arising from my deep understanding of the duality that underlies all of life. The poem also provides a picture of the intense energy that manifested in my immersion in the process of writing a book of poetry—literally creating something in the face of death.

Donald Wellman

ON AN EVENING

in New Hampshire, I slice citrus. Fresh juice has become a fetish,
sipped from a wine glass. My mornings are too hurried,
now that I am teaching.
I set the table with tangerine and lemon yellow china
made incidentally in Mexico.
The pattern is pleasing. I find patterns
among elements tossed together, verbal ensaladas
A sketch of a possible score in several parts: birds that share my thoughts,
dolls and pottery
glazed with a perfect azure, Puebla Talavera.

The song is an intimation of an end,
how a world that cannot not be sustained will find itself overturned
in a human tumult. Learn now
to appreciate a simple transition, a fortunate interim
in which to meditate upon dishes and beverages.

"On an evening" is from a poetry notebook entitled *Diario mexicano* (or Mexican daily with a pun on diary). An anthropologist of daily life, I have compiled several such notebooks. *Diario mexicano* is one of the three elements or sequences in the volume *Prolog Pages*, and the fact of belonging to a form of serial composition is important to the integrity of the text. It was written, it seems, upon return to New Hampshire after a stay in Mexico and reflects on the trip, sorting through things that in my imagination stand for ideas. For me, the writing of poetry involves the recognition of patterns, and that is what drove me to break the lines as I have and to conclude this poem as I have.

One subject in the collection is apocalyptic destruction, a theme that is very present in the words of "On an evening." There had been the Indian Ocean tsunami and the Mayan calendar predicts that our year 2012 is to be the end of time, a great tempest will erase the face of the sun. Isn't the idea of the sun and creation to be found on the face of one of those plates? My themes are destruction and the survival of children. It is that latter emotion that drives my poetry.

S Stephanie

WHAT THE NEWS SEEMED TO SAY

So easy for us to lose things,
and so many things for us to lose:

the wallet gone from the back pocket,
the car from the curb, a woman

and her child—yanked from the corner
like laundry from the line.

According to the newscaster, even our
tempers can be lost in plumes of "road rage,"

kick-the-dog rage, kill-the-boss rage;
dark clouds of pent-up anger, gathering

along the streets and arteries of America.
Fat clouds that can travel fast and settle

as far away as the Middle East. Now there's
a place where it rains heavily. Souls

rising like cheap umbrellas caught by wind,
dark balloons rising higher and higher,

leaving us little hope that someone
on the other side will find them.

And rain forests and dolphins seem to disappear
as easily as sunglasses and galoshes. Lost

dogs who can't smell their way back.
Homes to flood, Pictures to fire.

Wedding rings lost in all kinds of weather.
Memories locked behind broken neurons,

lives behind broken laws.
But some group in Nevada believes

they can save what's left with Anthrax.
Who knows what

they think they are saving. I don't
understand them. Today,

I spent the morning helping a woman
with Alzheimer's remember her husband's

name. She said it wrong, yet fiercely.
And she said it too loudly. The sound

of rocks hitting the bottom of a wheel-barrow.
As if the road she had been traveling before the war

suddenly ended. And now, the country
between them was impassable.

→

This poem came out of the frustration I sometimes feel when I watch the news. That feeling of one's hands being tied in the midst of so much negativity. It may have been my attempt at taking back my day. We do go on with the things we deem important, despite what is happening around us. At this time I was working with Alzheimer's patients. "What the News Seemed to Say" is also the title poem for my new chapbook. I put the chapbook together after realizing I was a bit of a "news junky" and had several pieces inspired by or incorporating news items in them. I then expanded on the theme of news to broaden the theme of the book.

Betsy Snider

OLD HOME DAY IN ACWORTH, 2008

The old man stares at the steeple
supported by new beams on the green.
He remembers their wedding day
as he looks up into the empty blue sky.

Supported by new beams on the green,
the steeple sits amidst pie sellers and soap makers.
The old man looks up into the empty blue sky
that arcs over the recently shorn church.

The steeple sits amidst pie sellers and soap makers.
Tables of books line the walk by the library
that squats beside the recently shorn church.
Children play next to the clapboard school.

Tables of books line the walk by the library.
He remembers their wedding day.
Children play next to the clapboard school.
The old man stares at the steeple.

I like to write form poems occasionally, when the form seems to fit the occasion. In "Old Home Day in Acworth, 2008," I used a pantoum. Pantoums seem particularly appropriate to capture an elegiac mood, steeped in nostalgia. There is something about the repetition of the sentences and the way the poem circles in upon itself that fits the character of old home days. In this instance, the steeple being removed added to the sense of both dislocation and the passing of time. The steeple on the Acworth church was taken down for repair two years ago. I am happy to report that it has just been restored to its rightful place, in time for this year's old home day in early August.

Ellen Hersh

MEMORIAL DAY PARADE

For Margery

Your knees all but
graze the slide
of your long brass trombone
as they rise
in time
beneath your purple mini.
Marching leftmost in the front row,
your knees
are knock knees,
my mother's knock knees.
Your name
my mother's name,
who loved parades,
the beat of drums
in her stomach.
Cymbals,
dogs' barks,
bike tires crunch on sand
as three stooped veterans,
buddy poppies trembling,
pass this lilac-shaded
bend of country road
leading you,
your horn,
your middle school band,
and row upon row of
young knees, lips, notes, bleats,
wails that shake the clouds,
scatter lilacs everywhere,
wakening the dead.

↦

"Memorial Day Parade," a poem from my chapbook, *Uncapping the Chimney*, shows how a chance sound, the beat of drums at a middle school parade, can trigger a series of images which build into a new vision, a synthesis of past and present, in the consciousness of the narrator. It also illustrates how a poet needs to stay limber to move backward and forward in time.

Marnie Cobbs

DIMINISHMENT

For my father during his depression

There are no blackberries there at all
behind the barn, thick with the brambles,
the leaping canes, the attentive thorn.
And after last year's abundance,
quart after quart, hours spent reaching in,
nudging, tipping, rolling them into your hand.
And none up the road, though
along the grassy trail by the lake
there were some, weeks ago—I picked a heaping
handful, carried them out in the front of my shirt.
Some years are like that.
Nothing where something used to be.

A few summers ago, my father took a fall, triggering depression, and within a
few weeks there was only an empty shell where his humor and energy had been.
The year before, we had had a banner year of berries out behind the barn, and
he had come out often to check on me as I gleefully picked and picked. We've
got him back again now, though I don't think he'd be interested in reading this
poem with its dark tone.

Martha Deborah Hall

THE SWING ON PEARL STREET

Once he's planed and varnished the swing seat, set galvanized bolts
      into the apple tree, strung ropes with grips that won't burn
      fingers, Dad declares it ready.
I learn the art of pumping.
Learn to fly
above the roof of the barn that lodges my horse and some bantam
      chickens;
above my grandmother hanging pillowcases on the clothesline;
above cornstalks drying in the autumn fields;
above the robins;

even above the wind.
Inside the house, mother plays Chopin, Dad drinks black coffee and
      puffs on a cigar. Knots under the sides of the cherry plank seat
      continue to hold as I make a safe landing.

"The Swing on Pearl Street" came to be written as part of my recent book *Two Grains in Time* published by Plain View Press in 2009. The book is dedicated to my identical twin sister, Kappy, who predeceased me in 2002. This poem takes place in a small Connecticut town, Seymour, back in the early forties.

Fred Samuels

STRANGE DUETS AND CITRONELLA

We would sit on the red brick porch
above the haze of Brooklyn's lights,
the summer stars sat neatly in place
while our neighbors played on their mandolins,
sang of Napoli, Sorrento, Roma;
here and there an errant star
would streak across the tidy sky.
Dad with eight-stringed banjo-mandolin,
sang from London music hall, from New York vaudeville.
Strange duets:
" . . . Some say the world is made for fun and frolic,
and so do I, and so do I . . ."
"Oh the moon shines tonight on pretty Redwing . . ."
The Ferraras invited us to share homemade
pizza and dandelion wine
so long ago in my improbable youth
by an earthen road in Flatlands
where neighbors had goats, grape arbors,
fig trees, tons of "egg tomatoes" for paste.
" Finniculi, finiculaaaaa . . ."
". . . her brave is sleeping while Redwing's weeping . . ."

"we sat tight and tense,
hushing the growling of our terrier
fearing that their fury might turn
toward the one Jewish family
in their midst."

In this first stanza of "Strange Duets and Citronella," Fred gives a vivid feel for
what life in his old Brooklyn neighborhood was all about—right down to the
sights, the scents, and the songs of it. His happy memories of growing up in the
old Italian neighborhood never left him. But there is also a final stanza of this

poem, where he paints an entirely different picture—the fights, the intolerance, the slurs, and finally, a little boy's fear.

These themes—peace and harmony versus chaos and intolerance—persisted throughout his writing career, perhaps in hopes that his poetry might help bridge the gap between the two.—*A friend of Fred Samuels*

Kyle Potvin

LOVE NOTE

Unseen, she tucked it in her lover's coat
while he was busy packing up his clothes
and laptop for a week away. The note
might be discovered on the plane. Who knows?
Or still much later in a hotel room
before he settles into bed alone.
Alone. She feels a sudden sense of doom
about things left undone and things unknown.
What if the letter falls out like a glove,
lost in a crowded airport ticket line,
then stamped by ruthless heels that can't feel love?
She wishes she had sent a clearer sign—
concealed her words where only he could see,
tattooed beneath his skin, indelibly.

When writing "Love Note," I was intrigued by this idea: What would happen
if an entire relationship hinged on the receipt of a single love note? Similar to
the premise in the movie *Sliding Doors*, there would be one outcome if the note
was read and an entirely different one if not. As often happens, I started writing
"Love Note" in free verse before deciding form, in this case, a sonnet, would
enhance the meaning.

Lesley Kimball

AFTER
For Adam

I am bowed over,
heavy with spent desire;
A milkweed pod split open,
scattering seeds;
the peony,
spilling ants
intoxicated.

I am hollow:
A cracked pottery bowl,
a stony summer stream bed.
My singular purpose
to be filled,
drained,
filled again.

I ring at dog frequency,
could be used to tune pianos;
wet fingers on the rim of infinite
crystal glasses.
The underground buzzing
of yellow jackets
shimmers on my skin.

I am built of the scent
of August marsh,
wishing well verdigris pennies,
the first turn of leaf-molded dirt.
Tongue-rich smells
permeate my fingertips,
behind knees, inside elbows.

I am nothing:
inside-out, undone;
the undeveloped negative,
the impression on the pillow,
the stillness of the curtain.

The early images for "After" came in the afternoon, in the bed I was sharing with my new husband—images that draw on the senses and memory to describe feelings that I had no words for. As the poem emerged, I tried to include all the senses in the images and in the experience of the poem ("buzzing," "infinite crystal") as well as maintaining the early connection to the natural world, an appropriately wild context for sexuality. Despite the first line of the second stanza, I didn't anticipate the stillness at the end of the poem. Sometimes, the poem knows more than we do.

Katie Umans

EKPHRASTICS

The brown house in yellowed landscape
is pure exercise in architecture,
portrait of land's thirst.

(What you cannot see:
a homestead woman
stands behind the house

killing sage chickens
with a shotgun. The painter
hates her heat

her bloodied hands
and patience, but she hates
her hunger more.)

      * * *

The woman at toilette:
a sheep white wisp
whose thoughts have always

rested lightly in her mind
like tortoise combs in piled-high hair—
she wanted nothing more or less

than what her watcher wanted
from her: hollow
of her throat, a face

to turn to mirrors, soft
anticipation of
the evening's entertainment.

(She did not want an infant
by her dressing table, the painter
sure to render it

the frail gray-white
of garlic with its
purple underbleed.)

     ★ ★ ★

The latest model arcs
on the divan.
(At home, in kitchen light,

the painter's wife
peels a thick neck
 of butternut for supper.)

The painter puts
the model's nakedness
into the horse's eye,

the one that's flickering
with nervous ignorance beneath
the hero braced for battle.

⇀

Ekphrastic poetry is traditionally poetry that comments on another piece of
art, frequently a painting. I have a love-hate relationship with ekphrastics. Art
bouncing off art can be interesting, but it can also be a cat chasing its own
tail. . . . I decided to try writing an ekphrastic poem that has no actual piece of
art as its subject at all. Its images are all invented or composited from the art I've
seen in my lifetime. I think that the poem is really about the conflict between
the intentions of the artist and the needs of real people.

Shelley Girdner

BROOD

For a few weeks, a blue jay boarded here
in the shag bark hickory, magnificent
even among the magnificent
of its species, large and wildly chevroned
blue and white and black. It attacked
any bird, any cat, bumbling human,
to protect its partner open beaked and on the nest.
The male and female jay are hard to tell apart
harder after the eggs have cracked, when
for a time, both parents feed the hatchlings
with the intensity of medics performing CPR,
hunting and shuttling back with the rhythm
of chest compressions. A part of me rises up:
Why do I hate the jays?

For a few weeks, the jays live so penitently
for one another and then nothing, that devotion
to a hunger outside their own, erased.
The parents fly off when the fledglings do,
slipping cleanly from the clutch.
If a parent jay were to meet its offspring later
in the wild, it might never know, might give chase
with that kind of dive-bomb anger I watched it train
on every other creature in protection
of the ones it made.

The Koran says everything is perishing
but God's face. I was thinking something else:
that love would last; my brood, my stab
at permanence. I found the blue jays' nest
blown free—a fleeting center, empty thatch,
a clump of hair pulled from a brush,
as dead as that.

~~>

In late May and June of this year, I watched a fierce blue jay chase after robins and oblivious pigeons. As I watched, I knew I was writing, though some underlying meaning remained hidden from me. I tried to coax it out: I wrote this as a prose poem; I rewrote it, removing the first person entirely; for a time, squirrels were involved. Then I took a day trip to Boston to watch in awe as my brother defended his dissertation in Religious Studies at BU. As he spoke, my poem came rushing back to me and suddenly I understood what had been lingering beneath my conscious understanding of the scene. This is why I love poetry, because so often when I have found the end of my imagination and comprehension, the world rears up and shows me a way.

Mary-Catherine Jones

SPIDER

eight legs,
you won
in a lottery,
spider.
strictly in
clined you are,
to tramp
led ambition.

but fast some
how fast
you take
curtsy, pir
ouette, leave.
have you
an audience
elsewhere? a
highway
of these
days. a
glass of you. of
you & i. spun out
on this wood
en stage, we are

soloists. & unlament
ing.

we God's
synonyms for
spider. so
many of you
with so many
eyes—how did
you purchase

the same numb
er of legs as
eyes? across
my cheek I
brush a
side a part
icle once liv
ing on a wood
en desert. there
are empty
tables every
where.

I was studying with Ilya Kaminsky, reading Paul Celan, working among a sea of wooden tables in a coffee shop. After mailing my month's work to Ilya, he sent it along to *Poetry International*—unbeknownst to me. Spider is my first published poem. Currently, I am striving to: read, think and write, improve the manuscript written during my time as an MFA grad, curate a reading series in downtown Keene, New Hampshire. I am eager to expose fresh and established talent to the Monadnock region.

William Doreski

PORTRAIT OF HART CRANE

Not only the open white shirt,
the undershirt collar showing,
but the crude texture of the face,
the boxer's nose swollen like
a drunkard's, the pores wide open
like portholes of the Orizaba,
from which he'd jump two years later.

Maybe for this one photograph
Evans used orthochromatic film.
Maybe exhausted by phone calls
from sloshed or overwrought Crane,
Evans decided to impale
instead of portray him. But really
it's the expression, the head turned

to his right, the eyes half-lidded,
the carved mouth carefully neutral.
Was Crane looking to someone else
for a cue? Or tired of facing
himself straight inside the lens?
No one has ever explained
these portrait sessions, but something

is brewing in that gaze: hurricane
below the horizon, "Sky-seethe,
dense heaven dashing;" or maybe
only that simple-minded drowning
that leaves the Atlantic quivering
after a sudden slack of tension
no one expects to survive.

→

A photograph of Hart Crane taken in 1930 by Walker Evans hangs above my desk. Crane is important to me not only because of the efficacy of his work but because the first published poet I ever met introduced me to Crane's poetry and gave me the old *Collected Poems*, edited by Brom Weber. This was my first book of modern poetry. Both Crane's work and life are exceptional and haunting. His death by water rebukes Eliot's abstraction in *The Waste Land* (section IV). It still lingers, as does Walker Evans's stark black and white America. The harsh enjambments and terse accentual rhythms of my poetry derive from Crane. I could never catch his immense compression, or the devious echolocation of his attenuated imagery, but I can at least quote it.

Alice B. Fogel

VARIATION 18: BAKER

Always daily in darkness deeper
than the former lit room of my dreams

I rise to predawn. By daybreak already
the bread side by side like cobblestones

baking in the great black womb,
its spirit scent ascending:

that sweetness that bitterness
absorbs and then sets free. Always already

the wheat in the field, hunger, rain.
The stalks in the bleeding

hand, grain
in the mill, chaff on the ground.

Grain ground until
all air's banished, all spaces fill

with the lighter heavier
powder of flour:

Then once more in the solid
dough, pushing, breath-infused, inspired,

the yeast singing from the heart
always already wine-alive,

releasing, like some tiny muse being
compressed, so the more I press, the more

it rises up—soprano prayer
returning to God and soon to be

folded into well-oiled forms. And by day
always already I have swallowed

steaming the broken
wholeness of fresh-grown loaves,

the aboriginal substance a language selved
warm in my throat, another

expanded breast's intake of air
firmed in the famished flesh.

In my full-length project based on Bach's *Goldberg Variations*, each poem speaks
from a different being or state of being, on a related theme of spirit and embod-
iment. Bach uses a double sixteen-measure structure, each meant to be played
twice; I use the same structure—two sixteen-line stanzas—with couplets to
mimic the two-fold aspects of both the form and the content. For #18, a canon
with overlapping, rising and falling "voices," this baker from some past century,
and his rising bread, came to me. I'm sure some bakers, then as now, are just
plain business-minded and not all that spiritual about getting up every morning
to punch dough, but that's why this one got the job.

Meg Kearney

HOME BY NOW

New Hampshire air curls my hair like a child's
hand curls around a finger. "Children?" No,
we tell the realtor, but maybe a dog or two.
They'll bark at the mail car (Margaret's
Chevy Supreme) and chase the occasional
moose here in this place where doors are left
unlocked and it's Code Green from sun-up,
meaning go ahead and feel relieved—
the terrorists are back where you left them
on East 20th Street and Avenue C. In New York
we stocked our emergency packs with whistles
and duct tape. In New England, precautions take
a milder hue: don't say "pig" on a lobster boat
or paint the hull blue. Your friends in the city
say they'll miss but don't blame you—they
still cringe each time a plane's overhead,
one ear cocked for the other shoe.

"Home By Now" is the title poem of my most recent collection, which seems
to have one foot planted in New Hampshire and the other in New York, where
I lived until 2005. I was living in Manhattan on September 11, 2001, but honestly
never thought I would write about that day. Yet a few years later echoes of it
started creeping into my work, and after a while I stopped trying to edit them
out. It's nearly impossible to be a writer living in this world and avoid writing
about the fact that we're at war; but it wasn't until this book came out and I
started reading the poems in public that I realized just how much the themes
of war and September 11 had woven themselves through so many of the poems.
Perhaps my being in New Hampshire was a sort of catalyst, as in many cases—
such as "Home By Now"—I thought I was writing about my new home state
and instead I was also writing about the place of my birth (much more than I
did when I lived there). Of course, there's nothing like leaving one's home for
another to bring on the question of what exactly "home" is, and when we know
we're there.

Don Burness

FALLEN SNOW

it has been many years
since I have spent a winter
in New Hampshire
a December snow
is burying the land
mallards dressed in flakes of white
decorate the lake
I had forgotten
winter in New Hampshire is beautiful
and beautiful you my dear
every season with you
has been a festival
now you are old and frail
in need of care
I look at you and I'm aware
how great it is to be alive
always a mixture
of the old and the new
and how blessed I've been
to share it all with you!

The very poor health of my wife Mary-Lou changed our lives. She needed twenty-four-hour care. For over a decade we spent winters in Portugal, but a stroke in early 2008 ended that stage of our life. In the winter of 2009 she was well enough to go to St. Augustine, Florida. So yesterday when the first snowstorm arrived, I was looking out on Lake Monomonac; I happened to be reading the poem "Fallen Snow" by Alykul Osmonov of Kyrgyzstan—and I looked at Mary-Lou lying on the couch—and I wrote this poem. Mary-Lou died January 5, 2015.

Dorinda Wegener

HOMESTEAD

The wind tugs the sweet gale; the pepperbush bobs in the thicket.

Ice thaws in the brook out back—
      mud-fossil footprints where the child ran,
      learnt the ways of serpent and bee.

      These were my fields.

March-bog where I nursed the lack
of barn swallows nested in rafters, away—

Why does winter return me?
To old, gray snow; white paint, ill and peeling—

      They have remodeled the front barn and the silo, clean gone.

Sentimentality—my small enchanter's
nightshade, you cliff seep my bones; leave me—
      these were My fields.

The jolt-April breeze disturbs; there should be no fear in this plot.

      I am no longer that wild button bush.

↝

"Homestead" was the first poem written after the MFA process. It began as a response to the debate on sentimentality and its role within poetry, but soon evolved into a direct, personal address to sentiments: love, pity, nostalgia, fear. As I wrote through the drafts, I noticed the images were representative of endings: graduate school; my childhood through my own child's growing; the loss of family and the definition of "family." Traveling through such melancholy, I knew I had to successfully ground the poem. New Hampshire, being my "home state," held the resolution: all the vegetation written into "Homestead" is native, a natural heritage to juxtapose my maudlin mind.

Linda Dyer

ARTIST UNDEFILED

Sao took up painting after she was pink-slipped
by the Thai timber company. Her time
no longer spent in hauling logs through forests,
she whiles away her days with brush
and canvas, slapping languid strokes of russet
across the taut stretched fabric, mixing in
a gentle curve or two of olive green
with now and then a splash of citron.
It matters not to her that her counterpart
in Phoenix pulls in a hundred grand a year
for her abstract expressions. Sao merely does
what she does and what she feels.
Let others detect the influence of her island youth
on Phuket, the style of her brushstrokes
so much like Gauguin. She is too thick-skinned
to be troubled by the critics.
She just paints and paints, unmindful
of the high-toned art historian's proclamation
that her art exhibits a maturity and depth unrivaled
by any of the other elephants who paint.

Like most people reading a newspaper, I zero in on what interests me and skip
the rest. Articles on art always catch my eye. In this case I happened on a profile
in the *New York Times* about an artist from Thailand. In reading about her, it
occurred to me that her approach to art is one that all those involved in the
creative arts should emulate.

Christopher Volpe

HOW IT IS

Sometimes the hummingbirds forget how to hum and fall like
multicolored comets flashing into the grass. That's how we lost our
wings too. Most anything falls often enough it breaks. This doesn't
stop us from exchanging keepsakes, because to cherish the smallest
gifts of the world as it could be makes it more convincing, more
joined, the way hands will when the bus is late and to be in line
together is all that matters. At the center of every childlike thought
there stands a ring of trust, within it only air. It isn't clear how colors
can be disturbing, but they can. Its humanity's rub, a wreath of wings,
a gift for making things important. Trading the plummet of the
songbird, say, for the minister's wife shooing kids from the desert table.
Look, young men shout things from the windows of passing cars:
here's one now, mouthing whatever, leaning Christlike, arms spread,
into the air.

"How It Is" used to be part of a manuscript of prose poems I was working on
called *Landscape with Lawn Ornaments*. The poems came out of a kind of paraly-
sis I felt coming of age on Long Island in New York, where nothing is as sensible
as anything in New England. The poems were a little bitter, I think; they with-
held meaning from the reader out of protest, or spite, or something. All I knew
when I was writing them was that I wanted them to read like surreal short-short
stories. The thing was, by their nature, poems like this lack emotional dynam-
ics; and as a manuscript, a whole book of them seemed too monotone, too flat.
So I abandoned them in a folder on my computer, and now and then, I rescue
one and begin editing it, playing around with it, "worrying" it, as they used to
say, like a predator with its hapless prey.

Ivy Page

ROOSTERS

We had four
shipped to us in a bunch
from the hatchery. At eight
years old on a farm
it happens . . .

The hatchet went through
the neck of the first, smooth and easy.
Blood spurted out
the body flew to the top
of my mother's car
parked halfway across the yard.

It flopped and sputtered, then suddenly . . . death
on the cream colored roof.
A bright red gush running down
the windshield.

You can only have one rooster.

"Roosters" is a narrative poem that is not only about roosters, but the way in which a young girl comes to understand the way relationships work. The beginning of the poem starts quietly giving the setting. In the second stanza we have the simplicity of the action of butchering chickens on the farm tangled with the subtle undertones of the first experience with a man, "The hatchet went through the neck / of the first smooth and easy." Not only does this describe the killing of a rooster, but also the emotional feelings of the first love lost. This piece was inspired by my childhood experience on a farm, and the complex nature of male/female relationships. It was written during my senior year at New England College's MFA program.

Anna Birch

INTO THE FOREST

We enter the company of these pines
and poplars, wander through this amphitheater
of curved earth, glacial remnants
that hold us in their dense worn shadow.

The old women in town
follow the wood roads in deep,
wade through ferns and laurel,
hover and bend
for mayflower blooms
uncovered from last year's leaves.

My mother searches for mushrooms here,
breaks me off a black birch sapling twig to chew,
shows me the poison nightshade berries,
the wintergreen berries,
teaches me how to choose.

We climb into the cellar hole
of the old Bailey place
that caught fire in the middle
of the night, the seven children
who raced into the moonlit woods
in weightless gowns and bedclothes.

Here is where we carved our names
into the bark, the grove where the boys in town
tried to take us on Friday nights.
Forest where we were shamed
and sustained, where we kissed and sang
and lost our breath,
and where my brother
has wandered off to again—
his pale, white legs
bright among the hushed and darkened trees.

"Into the forest" reflects experiences I had as a child with my family among the forests and woodlands surrounding our hometown of Hollis. My hope is that it taps into universal, archetypal aspects of life, how generations link and pass across time and the land's unspoken witness.

Christina N. Cook

NIGHTCRAWLERS

There's a Coltrane kind of smooth swing breeze blowing
through these oaks,
                                    high-brassed whines of a slow
moody sax, lips girdling woodwind reeds, *Green
Dolphin Street* slink

as black & white & blue in mood as this low grove
where the cold charity of dirt yields foot-long worms
                                    to our blunt spades.

Sharp Arcana jut
            from the moss: Star, Tower, Wheel

of Fortune, luck in the dark of our jazz
                        vespers, our trump-loaded houses of cards.

We find fontanels in the earth,
            fill Folgers cans with worms
                                    while filament-thin cicadas sing
"Blue Monk"
            to the bass voice of the bullfrog.
                        Their notes smoulder like a last glance
as we turn back toward our cottage.

                                    The lake is a Tarot tonight,
            full of Fools and Devils riffing
                        over the slow surface of cool blue.

→

"Nightcrawlers" is set at the old family lake cottage where I do much of my writ-
ing, and it posits a nighttime worm hunt with my sons. Like many of my poems,
the form is visually loose yet physically coheres in the same space that would be
taken up by uniform lines and stanzas.

First inspired by Charles Wright's long, seemingly loosely written lines, I have been working on this visual arrangement for some time, which fluctuates some with the particular needs of each poem. "Nightcrawlers" also speaks to the importance I place on musicality in my poetry. Jazz is a strong influence on my writing, and I try to structure my phrasing in terms of its rhythms and syncopation. I'm always looking for ways to bring in elements of the unexpected, which delights me in the music of John Coltrane, for example. In addition to unexpected rhythms and line breaks, I look for unexpected words, word-pairings, and elements, and for this I borrow liberally from the Tarot, Alchemy, and mythology.

Although my sons and I have never gone on a nightcrawler hunt and I don't practice the Tarot, the poem speaks to a certain reality of how it feels to walk through the woods by the lake at night.

Cleopatra Mathis

CANIS

It was a small comment, wasn't it, about who they were
—that last year on the dunes when all the town talk
was of coyotes, prairie wolf in search of an ocean,

those footprints instead of rabbits surrounding the shack
or half-sunk in the cranberry bog
just off the path. They heard the howling somewhere

behind their backs as they walked out past midnight,
singing at the top of their lungs:
abandon me, oh careless love—although they knew

the coyotes knew exactly where they were. No surprise
to either of them when they wailed unusually close
and loud on a moonless night after an argument,

this time a mean one about the dogs. For God's sake,
the dogs, how much trouble they were to him,
their feeding and whining and constant

need to go out, no matter how wet or cold. And so on
till silence set itself between them, holding stiff
as each turned away to bed. But the coyotes just outside

started up their merciless lament, as if
the entire genus called them, had bound the tribe together
in protest for their brothers. Hours they heard the keening,

both of them sleepless, that rising, falling
complaint in their ears—until he couldn't bear it, he said
I'm sorry, I can't do this anymore, and she in a rush

of understanding the exact suffering fit of it, jumped up
and closed the offending one window's
half-inch crack, and just like that

in the dead center of a moan, the coyotes
stopped their noise; what I mean to say is
the wind stopped making that heartbroken sound.

⟶

"Canis" is the first poem I wrote in a series about my most recent experience on the outer beach of Provincetown, Massachusetts. Coyotes have recently found their way to Cape Cod, and the poem introduces a central metaphor in my collection, *Book of Dog*.

I consider the poem a kind of gift because the precipitating event in the poem happened just as it's described. I'm not usually so lucky that a poem seems to write itself, as this one did. But I find that metaphor is very sneaky: it finds us in the fabric of our lives; we don't invent it.

Mary Spofford French

THE MAGIC SHOW

We would walk to the rail road station
then hop along the platform while mother
straightened her hat and checked to be sure
The Pass was in her purse, because
that meant we rode the B&M for free,
because our daddy owned it.

Well, of course he didn't, but for us
he did. Especially after we were seated
on the red velvet in the passenger car
and the conductor would come in at one end,
along with sooty smoke, calling out
Tickets! Tickets Please!

At that, our mother would reach deep
into her bag to pull out the square of print
that made us special. We were headed for Filenes
that magnet for mothers who shopped
in the Basement. A grey and white place
where heating and plumbing pipes
criss crossed just under the low ceiling.

Where women jostled in their rayon slips
to try on dresses from the racks and in
narrow spaces between low tables where
bargains were mounded in tangled piles.
Being not quite five my eyes were just about
level with the edge of one. I watched
as silk scarfs threaded themselves up

the wide sleeves of a black coat. No sooner
had they vanished when a purple dress
with blue flowers followed. Next were silk
stockings and a pink laced up girdle

with those metal things that dangled
and glittered, and then a bright red nightgown.
Too soon the woman in the black coat
stepped back and disappeared.

This poem is a memory, a reminder of how children see.

Mary Ann Sullivan

DAVID AND GOLIATH

I will take one small stone
and I will stand before the giant
who threatened so many

and while the crowd screams,
goads on
mocks

with experience gained alone
at my leisure
with a solitary sling

I will in a short moment
To the forehead
Send a stone
Direct

There

And then
And then

Having felled the glumox

Continue
at my leisure

to right
to writing
write
right

I wrote "David and Goliath" at a time when the pressures of life were hindering my ability to write poetry. For me, old testament figures serve as symbols and metaphors. In this case, Goliath symbolizes all that hinders me from creating, whether it be actual human beings, the business of life, or my own personal flaws. With this poem, I confront and slay the giant.

Sara Willingham

PHOTOGRAPHING THE SUNSET

Chamberlain Lake is huge this year,
the gray shale beach
is buried under water,
so I sit on the bank
beneath a circle of birches,
dangle my feet
and take portraits of the sky.

All around me, like grief
which never goes away,
are the photographs I don't take:
the bent silhouettes
of pewter trees,
a scrawl of moose tracks
spilling over with rain.

I shoot another roll of film
and hope for an epiphany.

It takes hours.

Above Mt. Katahdin
clouds break into ruddy imaginings,
the aging sun hangs in the cove
like an empty sleeve.

Out on the deepest part
of the lake, where amethyst swells
release their hold
and turn back toward shore,
a man gives his father's ashes
back to the wind.

Nugent's Camp, the Allagash

Some years ago I spent a week in the Allagash at a wilderness location accessible only by boat. One evening I sat by myself on the graying dock that leaned out into the lake, and I watched the entire sunset from the first hint of color until I was wrapped in the darkness. I had never taken the time to watch an entire sunset before, and as a photographer I was fascinated by how many changes took place within the span of only a few minutes.

When I sat down later to work on "Photographing the Sunset," I was thinking about the owner of the camp where I stayed that week. He had recently lost his father and had described to me how he'd scattered his father's ashes out on the lake. This poem, like many or perhaps even all poems, is also about the act of writing: sometimes, after shooting a few hundred photos, we come up with a single great image. Sometimes, after rewriting many drafts, we write a poem that leads us to a discovery both universal and particular to our own mythology.

Katherine Morgan

ACCOMPLICE

Bermuda grass pokes our knees,
damp night air presses our t-shirts to our backs,
as crickets chirp on the firebreak.
Between us and the ocean, black in the distance,
lemon groves fill the valley
with wax-white blossoms
and the fragrance of spring.

With a sudden pop, the BB rips the lily pad
where once a peeper sat.
Another "troublesome" voice will sing no more.
Belly up, it floats, legs spraddled,
inside my circle of flashlight.
My brother collects the specimen
with a bounty hunter's grin.

I imagine pennies clinking into my bank
and try not to look.

This poem grew out of an experience with my older brother when we were
kids growing up in southern California. We lived in the foothills of the Santa
Ynez mountains, and could see the ocean three miles away. The sights and
smells of the California landscape have stayed with me though I have lived in
New England for over forty years. I have always loved the Italian sonnet form,
but never use the strict formal elements. This poem includes the "turn" that
happens between the octave and sestet of an Italian sonnet, but that is its only
resemblance to the sonnet form.

Kelly M. Flynn

FIRST AMPHORA

Odysseus opens the first amphora on his return to Ithaca.

But first sleep: a still white lamp, a nurse
whose white palace hand may calm the dark wave

of the rough sails home,
the rough swims.

Then you rise and go down to the dark,
to the jar sealed against the hour,

tall stone curves cut from your stone island,
two-armed and coolly sensual, royal and guarded

by a tall woman. You probably know
she did it for herself, you know

you will join together then each return
to the vigil over the other's isolation;

she knows she is not what
you returned for, nor even your child,

brave dividend you could not watch watching
it all again through sun-white eyes that burned

your eyes to look into and so you sailed away.
Walk down these stairs into the dark now

and know: so many years ago there was wine
in the amphora, but now maybe only

spider bodies piled in a knot of death, pebbles
from your sandals, a scoop of ashes, a darkness

that can never unfold itself, a handful
of dry salt, a cool pile of moonbeams shrunken

into twigs. You were away from yourself
longer than you know. Then see

what you find when the beloved
with her long arm prizes open, ringingly,

the marble in the cool zone under the world.
It is a history of self solved in blood,

arterially red and war-bright once, but lapsed
and cooling even from your youth,

wine-dark from way back,
the sea you sailed out and home on.

I wrote "First Amphora" a few years back after reading *The Odyssey* for the first time, and found that after my father died last year, I wanted to return to it and edit it. This gave me an opportunity to contemplate at greater length the central image of Odysseus returning to his home after a twenty-year journey and open-ing the first of many amphoras to drink the wine he had stored in them before he left. That image has its hooks in me as a representation of the mystery of the question of what an individual life amounts to at its end, of how we appear to ourselves when we return home, so to speak, after all our battles.

Roberta Visser

WISH

For my grandson

What I wish for you is time
to sit in the light of the kitchen and your mother
moving around talking to you,

to be lulled by guppy waves lapping against the rowboat
while the sun reflects itself in placid patches of water, and shadows
a swath of pointed pines on the edge of the shore.

Sitting here, I remember my mother saying, *I just want to sit, quiet.*
Like her, I want to take time in sunlight, in silence,
to watch birds flit rapidly from branch to branch, calling out

for reasons I do not know, while clumps of snow fall
from pine bough and hemlock branch to make their own prints
as prominent as those of the night feeding deer.

Sitting here, I can feel my heart beating
aware that I am for you, the repository of memory,
I, a sometimes shepherd of my children,

in the larger sphere of nephews and their children,
all of us like stars splayed in the Milky Way,
bound by the desire to keep traveling together.

It's as if there is sinuous fiber, much like an umbilical cord, that attaches me to
my grandson, daughter and mother. The poem describes, if I could have my
wish, the secure and calm scenes I would lay out for my grandson in which to
live his life. Yet there is a larger circle of family—all the children, including my
son, nephews and their young—to whom I have a responsibility. That is, I must
pass on the legacy of my grandparents who brought to this country the ways of
the culture from which they came, and the spiritual traditions passed to them
over generations.

Ewa Chrusciel

NA   NO   LA

They thistle in us. They speck in the morning. They tingle. Sorrelic
apparitions. There is a tigress mother wanting to trim your hair. They
come to us. Do you hear them? Some as heavy footsteps. Others—
miniscule kisses. Thin as grass. Rising and swaying parasols. They
come with swinging hips. They come as minnows. They try to get
where they belong. They come in wrinkles. They come as a host of
molecules. They come as hard-faced dybbuks. They swarm into this
lighthouse. They have fancy hats. With forget-me-nots. They pebble
across the floor. They fall from marigold trees and lie crucified on the
road. Get up and sing. They pinch like too much love. They trespass.
They arrive at a wailing wall. They dot. We are burying them every
day. We are burying them in staccato rhythm. They rise and accrete.
They beat electric letters in the air. They hop always to a higher
branch. They come invincible. They come to torture. They come to
soothe. They come for romance. They flip and tremble tiny farewells.
They come as mustards seeds. Do you see them in a mulberry tree?
They slide down the needles. They come as growth on wolf trees,
the dead winking. They air the air. They come to forgive. They ask
for forgiveness. They come as hyphae. They come as hostages. They
come as clogged streets. They come in slow trains. They come as silver
jaguars. Burning bushes, doves, manna, the blood of horses' necks.
They come as purgatory souls. They chip off the wall. In loops and
whorls. They want to rent one line. They want to break down. They
recolonize. They come to insulate us with snow. They come in giggles.
They come in almonds. They come to eye us, inside our panther skins.
We bury them. They come in black chadors. They rap on our door
with churned up grains, tides, whispers. They come as drafts of juni-
per. They spread on the floor as a cross. They are relics of grief and
light. They perch on branches like monk hedgehogs. They come as
juncos. They come in lekking crowds. They come in high-strung beads
and scatter into our vessels. They come in volcanic lavish. They come
as noble Odysseuses. They hover as hummingbirds, calculating their
rates of return. We bury them. They air the air. They are ubiquitous as
Tartar cheeks. They bilocate. They come as yellow secrets.

→

The poem, "Na no la," is an accretion of various lines and themes from my 2011 book *Strata*. "Na no la" is a haunted poem. It is inhabited by the lines and images that emerge and expand throughout my book. They perch on a log and pound. They form a drumming station. They become a ruffed grouse. Pounding its wings until the forest hears; until the logs spark into lumen.

By embracing both mourning and abundance, this poem also alludes to the title of my book, *Strata*, which signifies "loss" in Polish and "accretion" in English. *Strata* investigates the issues of bilingualism; the ceaseless border crossing, smuggling of metaphors; inhabiting two places at once. It claims that poetry dwells in impossibility and bewilderment. It expresses longing for bilocation. It recognizes the insufficiency of one language; the human desire and inability to express the ineffable. "Na no la" distills and condenses these overarching themes.

Matt Jasper

TRIBUTARY

Aged two and three—
they seal-slide toward the sunlit top
of a stream that froze then lowered
a foot to freeze again beneath
its higher ceiling.

Their father startles then recalls
it's been cold too long for them to be taken
by the water beneath. Cautious
of caution, he sends
no warning to the delighted pair
as they smash through sparkling almost-glass
and discover these things:

They are still alive; they never knew
there could be ice beneath ice, that something thin
could smash them down to something holding firm
the memory that it once babbled and soaked.

By lying on their backs and pushing with their heels,
they can just fit under the sheet—
looking up through a craggy lens into a smeared sky
of lit branches iced also into conspiracy
smashed by laughter as sons destroy
the glory of a quarter mile—sliding under like torpedoes
slowed by the lifting shark fin of a knee.

When they see that propelling themselves cracks the sky,
they flatten and lie there chewing watery shards,
spitting out wool mitten fibers, demanding
that he push them farther than he dares—
each time closer and closer to beyond
where he hopes they will rise up
and return to him only
to be launched farther away.

When at last they slide
then creep around a bend
and don't come back to him,
he learns to trust that their screams
are joyous though reminiscent
in pitch to those of eviscerated swine.
The stream is frozen, he reminds himself.
There's no need to tell them not
to get carried away.

I wrote this poem ten years after a walk in the woods with two of my children. I often relived that day in memory and then cursed the sad fact that I hadn't brought a camera. Recently, I decided to just daydream my way back there and take a few snapshots with my memory. These glimpses brought the brilliant light of that day back and helped me reflect on how my children were changing—perhaps needing me a bit less, or differently.

Dudley Laufman

SHE TELLS US OF HER BROTHER'S PASSING

It was at church during time of sharing
in front of the entire congregation.
She whirled like a dervish, skirts a-flaring,
her face in radiant pure elation.
She said " I was out working the garden.
The sky was clear blue, the day was silent.
Suddenly without any warning,
a wind came roaring down upon the moment."
She twirled around and round, her hair was flying.
She said "It whooshed and whooshed and kept on whirling.
Picked up the hay mulch from its winter lying,
and carried it away, a twister twirling
up above the trees into the sky.
It was my brother come to say goodbye."

Jacqueline's older brother died recently in California. She had not seen or really
heard from him for thirty-five years. The poem came from what she shared
with us at his east coast memorial service.

James Harms

A WOODEN HORSE

We tied ropes and pulled.
It rolled a little, and then enough
to cross the drawbridge,
which we drew back shut and locked
with iron rods. Nick and Sally
climbed the tower and crouched
low behind the parapet to take
their turns watching the east,
from whence cometh nearly
every one we've ever hated.
We'd heard the rumors and
knocked. But the thing was
all echoey and empty, though
inside we found flowers
and enough red wine to
tip the town into dreams
of poppies and fair
weather. Salvador sang
"The Ballad of Queenie
and Rover" while Ted sliced
the ham and spread mustard
on bread, and Evangeline
for once let down her black
braid and taught the kids
the cha-cha. We were ready
when they charged, daisies
behind our ears. "Whosoever
steals will be blinded," Jamal
cried, as if reading from
the dictionary. Salvador
kept singing and we offered
the immigrants leftover
salad and what little
ham remained. "It was better

before we were barbarians,"
Franny whispered.
But they'd given us the wine
and wrapped it in wood,
and sent us a hollow horse
to hold our dreams in case
our hearts, at last, were full.

I love the song "A Wooden Horse" by the brilliant band British Sea Power (I've
made it the ring tone whenever my wife calls), so the poem began as a response
of sorts, a way of answering one work of art with another. It quickly became an
excuse to fool around with a bunch of anachronistic details and names, some-
thing I think poems are particularly adept at doing. Naturally, like British Sea
Power, I'm using a classic trope to explore contemporary notions, but in my
case the poem eventually evolved into a quiet (I hope) statement on immigra-
tion policy, something poems are *not* particularly adept at doing. Oh, well. The
poem also references Cavafy, Salinger and Stevens, but I hope not in ways that
are particularly noticeable.

Priscilla Burlingham

RENEWAL

All week the wind
redundant
a chorus of homeless leaves
blown and reblown
like paper lemmings
coughed up
from ground
to nickel light

On metallic rivers
the sky has frowned
for days
signaling fish
rubied and green gold
to scrape plump bellies
of roe and milt
their fry to sway
in jelly wombs
on stone

And undisturbed
in his mineral keep
the scarlet newt surrounds
his fingerless nub with cells
of pink
lush and safe with growing
as if the dark
was all he needed
to be immortal

This poem came out of a great respect for creatures whose energies are best spent on survival to replenish. It is easy to see why they were mythologized as symbols of power and hope and when we pay attention we may find they are guiding us still.

Bill Gleed

LABYRINTH

I take three steps into a labyrinth,
And am lost implacably, immediately.
I grasp indifferent phantoms. They
Glide like ice skaters round the pond,
Released like inane, dubious totems.

Here are possibilities of all that is and was and will be
In no straight lines and all straight lines:
Sunbeams spray from behind your head so I see God
Tilting over with his hand outstretched, the host
In his palm.

This is truth, golden and pure.
Errors and expectations, an invisible man, inventions
The stranger, leaf and bone and flesh
Imprecations strewn about the path, the labyrinth in which I am lost,
Thinking.

And you, God, withdraw from me
One minute more. I learn by heart to mouth the words
Crawling on my knees, cobblestone supplicant,
Endless sinner, impudent regressor ordinand.

Yet there is no trial balance, the host recedes,
No suture facile to staunch the flow of my blood
While beach plums redden their white flowers.

This poem, "Labyrinth," was written a couple years ago when I was at a cross-roads. The poem comes from that lost feeling that I think we all feel at times, when others and even institutions like the church offer advice on how to proceed, and fall short. In the end there might not be any resolution to whatever problem you find yourself dealing with, but life goes on around you.

Charles W. Pratt

OUT OF WORK

On May 11 of this, our last year in the orchard, a freeze destroyed the crop.

All summer the apple trees flared buoyant
In the absence of apples. Branches reached up,
Reached out; the mower passed easily under.
Leaves grew broad and abundant. We thought
Of Sundays in well-kept parks, picnics
On the grass, beauty without function,
Unless to be beautiful itself is function,
And felt ourselves vacant—the more so for knowing
That though the branches waved in unison
Like bleachered baseball fans, fat buds
Studded them; they were already at work
Making next year's harvest, next year
When the great gate shuts us out to wander,
Gardener groundless, poet with no theme.

For the past twenty-seven years my wife and I have owned and operated Apple
Annie, a small pick-your-own orchard in Brentwood. But I am about to become
a former apple-grower also, as we are in the process of selling the orchard to
another couple in order to ensure that it continues to provide pleasure and good
fruit to the community.

"Out of Work" is my most recent poem; what is said above and in the epi-
graph will explain how it came to be written.

Rodger Martin

AFTER CARL ERIK LUNDGAARD'S "VALSEN TIL CHRISTINE"*

Like the dusk call of parents
gathering again their important things,
summer rain drips from the deep eaves
soothing backdrop for darkening green.
A father balances a daughter in his arms.
They eddy like a quiet river about the promenade.
A planet rests on his shoulders.
He knows where the river flows:
the puppy clambering the peak of a flooded home,
the pelican flapping useless wings,
the great white bear, quizzical at its shrinking floe.
An accordion, skiff of the ancients,
skims the soft liquid of a violin—
so needy, so needed, crossing
the lost waters of this earth.

*Christine's Waltz

I regularly listen to Danish Radio on my computer, particularly the folk and world music channels. One day I heard Carl Lundgaard's "Waltz for Christine" and it immediately brought vivid images of a father waltzing in the rain with his four-year-old daughter across the large, wooden deck of a vacation spot on a bay or lake or river. In particular, the images brought back my own daughter at four, and my own childhood innocence and the heartache of a parent's ultimate inability to protect a child from the ravages mostly we, ourselves, loosed upon this earth.

As I heard the waltz again over a period of time, the images became more forceful and the music almost haunting, insisting I respond in writing to the world around me—Katrina (but as much the Great Flood of 1927), the BP oil spill (or as much the Exxon Valdez or Torrey Canyon), the humanity-caused warming planet. This poem was that response.

After the poem evolved, I decided I must have the CD as well, and in my internet research to purchase it (only available then in Europe) I found an English translation of Lundgaard's liner notes about the song. I was surprised (since there are no lyrics) to find the emotions that had driven him to write the music paralleled the language images his music had evoked within me. He had written it for his own daughter, who had left him as a teenager to travel to El Salvador and Guatemala to serve as a human shield to protect the peasants against the corporate abuse rampant in Latin America. There are some YouTube versions of the accordion, but the version which influenced me is with an accordion and violin on Lungaard's CD *Yderland*.

Scott T. Hutchison

SPECIAL DAY

At day's end most of the other kindergartners
took their cups of sweet butter
and raced to mommies' vans
to show off what they'd made.
A kindly crinkle-eyed farmer with a beard
and a churn had visited with us, explaining
grass and feed, Guernsey cow and milk,
elbow grease and a steady beat,
separation and the blessing of butter.
We all took turns making the world sweeter.
We plastic-spooned our creation out and onto
Mrs. Whitten's homemade bread
warm from a cafeteria oven, giggling
with bright liquid gold dribbling
down our chins. I loved Special Day,
never wanted it to end. The pick-up mommies
cruised in, cooed and clapped in wonderment
at the delights before them, happy that
the time apart was over and everyone
could return home to sugar and salt,
to cuddle and tuck. I stayed behind
and talked with the bearded man until
he claimed he had to go, switched to
Mrs. Whitten who checked the clock
and called Guidance for help
getting me on the short bus, a counselor
actually ordered to ride with me as I
kicked her shins; she took it
all the way to my stop before
prying my fingers from the seat's metal framing
by greasing them with butter and sliding
me down the steps and out
the doors to stand before my own dark
churning house, my cup empty
and crushed on the ground.

→

Teaching is complex—we know what occurs in our classrooms, but the insights we get into our students' lives away from school are often scant. We do the best we can, and we try to make our classes a place of both learning and refuge. Though some of this poem is fictionalized, not all of it is. This was sparked by a true story.

Kathi Hennessy

ANAMNESIS DIFFRACTED
For Kathy Szostak

To say how it was there should be music, a song of joy
ripe with color, like Paul Simon's *Kodachrome*:
the bold abundance of forsythia growing over the fence
into tunnels wide and brightened by our thronged
imagination, the cerulean of skies wide open enough
for any dream to dare, the air that smelled of green
and brown, the weeds and dirt, the stuff of whatever stuff
we were transmogrifying those days of dirt, playing
where no grass would grow, her seven siblings
plus always me, too much to compete with;
and reds, lots of wide-mouthed braying laughter,
skinned knees and carnival balloons, the hollow
orange *sproing* of a basketball bouncing infinity,
even gray, the rumble as garage door windows rattled
to its tune, the dust of boredom, hazy lurking skies
making summer overlong; yes even the lurid plaid
of our Saint Rita's jumpers, Peter Pan-collared necks
wrung by blue bow ties, the ties that bind—but not

the sepia haze of too much time gone by, of things too worn,
too old or dulled for memory to light, nor the black indelible ink
of our mortal sin, a danger, nuns informed, forever preying
on our souls, the bloodblack sin we carried with our books,
that funereal tone I could not bear, not for her; nor white,
the bleached-boned pale of antiseptic standard, the colorless
blank stare we were taught to cherish, born already smudged.
Picture her, transistor to one ear, *Kodachrome*'s kaleidoscopic riot
diffracting all the world into sunny days as yet unnumbered.

→

This poem arose out of personal tragedy. In 1993, my childhood best friend passed away at the age of thirty-two. We were in the same grade at the same school, had the same name, the same chicken pox scars. Though we had fallen out of touch, I was devastated by her passing. She and her brothers and sisters had been my childhood playmates for many of my earliest years, and the fond memories I have of that time in my life are owed largely to the Szostak family.

The poem began as my way of coping with her loss. I could not control fate, or even my own emotional response, but I could impose order on the words I used to write about her. I didn't want the poem to be about me, my grief, or even specifically about the loss of her, but about those childhood days full of magic and color, and sometimes fear and shame (given that we attended Catholic school in the mid-1960s).

Todd Hearon

LONGING SONG

That enchanted door between us, I'll never open it.
You will never step inside. We won't live
for a thousand years like the Arabians knowing everything
the garden of sensual gratification can supply.
You won't rise in a morning when the crocus comes
and leave me for the sun. There will be no more suns.
There will be no earth, no myths, no stories.
We will never be greater strangers to one another.
Happiness, contentment, those illusory lasting treasures,
these will not touch us. Loss will not
live as it did for us in our time.
We had no time. We'll never die.
The locket I gave you, the ring of fire, the silver cord,
all the photographs destined for our children never
pass into being, nor do our children.
None of this will have happened. We will never forget each other.

I was reading somewhere about the peyote religion as practiced by a certain
tribe in the American Southwest and how, in preparation for the "hunting" of
the mystical plant, members will speak using only negative statements for a
period of days. I thought, well there's an idea: try writing a poem using only
negative statements.

Martha Carlson-Bradley

FROM *IF I TAKE YOU HERE*

Back again at this back door.
As the cold of the metal latch
sinks into finger joints
it's November, maybe March—
leaf mold scenting the chill.
Only winter birds are speaking,
their insights brief, and sharp.
Is anyone home? Can I come in?
The spring on the screen door
stretching out
                    plays its taut,
ascending scale.

I first got the idea for the poems in *If I Take You Here* after seeing Jane Kenyon
and Donald Hall interviewed by Bill Moyers back in 1993. Hall's good fortune
as a poet in being able to live in his grandfather's house brought home to me
afresh the loss of my own grandparents' house, which was torn down shortly
after my grandfather died, when I was eleven. I can visit that house only in
memory, and all the poems in this collection are written as though memory is
a physical place we can visit—but that is still subject to all the uncertainty and
shifting qualities of memory.

Jennifer Militello

A DICTIONARY AT THE TURN OF THE MILLENNIUM

Hello to devouring, hello to digest,
to the end of lostness and the chill of less.
Hello to living like sardines.

To solace. To the offspring of hello.
Hello to desperation. Hello to welcome in.
Hello to generations that etcetera as we watch.

Hello to experiment with us.
Hello to angels at the mouth-ache
of more. Hello to the surgical morning.

Hello to the delicious red let of lakes,
to being gone like a long underwater.
Hello, it is an ordinary world, hello

limited time and autumn's pent-up monsters.
Hello, routine. Paralysis. Paradise.
Adrenaline catastrophe. Hello.

"A Dictionary at the Turn of the Millennium" reflects on the mass consumption
and relentless overpopulation that have come as a result of the voracious appe-
tite of the collective human machine. It repeatedly greets a future that is shaped
by our present communal acts and desires. The poem comes from a new manu-
script I'm working on, tentatively titled *A Camouflage of Specimens and Garments*,
the third and final book in what I consider the "identity trilogy" of my first
three collections. The book is made up of a series of ventriloquisms in the form
of "dictionary" poems written in the voices of ancient goddesses and long-dead
composers, mythological heroes and murdered girls, those selves shifting and
slipping away as facets of the disguises we all wear.

Pat Parnell

KOKOPELLI LEADS THE DANCE

My lover leaps, *en grand jeté,*
to join me on this mountain top,
dancing to the notes
of the hunchback piper perched
on a nearby cloud,
the notes I cannot hear.

Never a dancer, body intimidated
by fear of the flesh, he chuckles at the fun
of his new flexibility. His balance back,
he rises, bending the toes, *demi-pointe,*
that would not bend.
Brace and foot drop forgotten,
he pirouettes, grinning, showing off.
"Look what I can do," his smile says.

Led by the music he loved,
the agile piper beckoning, dancing ahead,
he gives me a last wave, then
takes double-somersaulting leaps,
cloud to cloud, 'til he is lost
to my sight. I hear his laughter, echoing
in zigzag ricochet, until that too is lost.

I whisper "good-bye," turn to go.
A slant of sunlight pierces the clouds,
lightens my way.

My husband Bill was a strong supporter of my poetry. When he passed away in
January, 2010, I wanted to find a way for us to say goodbye to each other through
poetry. Bill was a talented, self-taught photographer who enjoyed experiment-
ing with his photos, especially with composites. One of my favorites—posted

on our refrigerator for several years—was a silhouette of Kokopelli, the Native American hunchback flute player, leader of the dance, set against a cloudlike background. Studying Bill's photograph, I imagined Kokopelli as the Native American divine spirit who leads the souls of the deceased to the next level of their existence.

Mimi White

HE HAS WIND IN HIS HEAD

Sir, if you could fly over Vitebsk on the red rooster,
if you could milk a cow in the eye of a horse,
if the goat in the moon were your stone tablets,
you would know that ardor defies gravity
and that even the tiniest shoe spins like the earth
if it is fixed to the heart
of the man and the woman.
Your laws cannot explain why I sing
when a rooster crows my name in Yiddish
and when my father returns home
smelling of herring and sawdust.
Here's a fish and a slender horse,
a clock and a crucifix,
a fiddler with a purple cape.
Do only numbers explain mystery?
What equation proves that when a village
is obliterated there is madness loose in the world?
My home is smoke. Bella's white dress my crown.
When I swim with Bella on the ceiling
her hips are my eyes, my arms her breasts.
What else could bodies in love be
but each others' and the blue violin?

Last year I took a wonderful Ekphrasis Poety class taught by Kimberly Clout-
ier-Green. Kimberly asked us to write a poem in the voice of a painter we
admired. I chose Chagall, whose work has always fascinated me for its lightness
and its aura of love. Kimberly also asked that this be a poem of address to some-
one the painter might have a quarrel with or need to say something to. I chose
Sir Isaac Newton for obvious reasons, I hope.

Nancy Stewart

THE NINTH WAVE

Wave after wave, each mightier than the last
Till last, a ninth one, gathering half the deep . . .
—From Idylls of the King, by Alfred Lord Tennyson

My arm, at night,
resting on your chest
moves up and down.
Fast and choppy
at first, like wakes
made by motorboats.
Then slower,
like Oregon hemlocks
we've stood under
as they swayed.
A whole forest of them
in unison.
Until only my hand
rises and falls
like driftwood
over swells. You rest,
I lie, awake and still
counting your breaths,
imagining
the ninth ones
are deepest.

This poem, "The Ninth Wave," began at the ocean near Tillamook, Oregon.
Too cold for swimming, but warm enough to stay awhile, I noticed some waves
were much bigger than others and started counting those in between, thinking
there might be a pattern. My father-in-law, who had served in the Coast Guard
during WWII, was with us and when asked, thought it was either the seventh
or the ninth ones that were supposed to be the biggest. My observations that

day were inconclusive. However, like seeing pregnant women everywhere you go when you're pregnant, the next week I came across an article about scientists who had debunked the belief in common lore that in a series of ocean waves, the ninth waves are biggest. A survey of my Robert Graves books and the *Dictionary of Phrase and Fable* also turned up some references to ninth waves.

A little time spent daydreaming and I had the start of a poem. I placed the poem in Oregon, both because that is where it germinated and, since it's a love poem, because my husband is from Oregon. Once I had finished the poem, I sent a copy to my sister in London. A couple of weeks later, on a business trip to Russia, she found herself going through a package of postcards she'd bought at the State Russian Museum in St. Petersburg. There, spread out on the bed, to decide which to send to whom, was Ivan Aivazovsky's 1850 painting of a boat in a rough sea titled, *The Ninth Wave* (1850).

Harvey Shepard

THE TENDERNESS OF MEN

It's in the way he lifts his chin
and sets his head firmly
on squared shoulders
as if to confirm
his right to occupy space
before moving forward.

It's in the way his eyes
do not see, his gaze
turned inward, searching
for reassurance, a renewal
of strength to do battle
in the world of men
and desirable women.

It's still deeper:
in heart and lungs and gut,
in the secret desire
within chest and arms
fingers and face
to be held
—to touch and be touched.

The basic aim of my poetry is to explore the mystery of being a human being.
I wonder about and am fascinated by how people live, what they think about in
private moments and in relationships, what makes life worthwhile for them. I
feel that we communicate so little of this inner life to others, even family and
friends, and believe it is a primary source of the loneliness and anxiety most of
us experience. This poem began while I was sitting at South Station in Boston
waiting for a train to New York, observing people walking by.

Lin Illingworth

ON THE DAY BEFORE YOU WERE BORN
To Jack

Your grandfather and I rode bikes through
an alley of trees and called their names
to each other, Latin spindling into the wind—
> *Acer saccharum*
> > *Betula populifolia*
> *Pinus strobus*

Syllables clicked from our mouths
like baseball cards clothes-pinned
to the bikes' bright spokes; even the sun
clicked from The Lion to The Virgin
under unending sky so soon shot through
by planes headed toward you—
Everything took the day off to get ready
for your arrival; maybe my father's cancer cells stopped
reaching their spindles toward each other and forgot,
for an hour, their multiplication and division, another thing
we will teach you, like how to ride a bike through
a tunnel of green toward some bright end,
that the moving shadows along the path are made
of simpler things—maple, beech, pine—that all
of it belongs to a family, a genus, a species, a sky
and all at once is singular: this day, the moment
you enter, your name held in the wind's mouth,
wheel-round and full of some new story.

This poem arrived while working a prompt to include unknown words in
a poem—hence the Latin, but—in truth—the more pressing reality of a
step-daughter in labor with a first grandson, as the poem was being written,
colored everything. The day before, as my husband and I stopped our bikes
every half-hour to check our e-mail for updates, I kept thinking how the green
tunnel was a sort of birth canal. The scope of that, coupled with a visit days
before to my father as he was getting ready for chemotherapy, had me thinking
about how it is all happening, all at once.

John-Michael Albert

BLACKBERRIES

It was a ploy, of course. One of mom's tricks.
Take your cousins down to the ditch and
bring back some blackberries for desert.
And we were off with plastic butter tubs
(leaving the aunts and uncles talking
on the porch, the rotisserie tumbling
over the coals, the ice-cream churn humming
to beat the bees), with no thought of returning
because we were happy, and we were with friends.

Then, in the ditch (squashing the late
mulberries under our bare feet, yearning
for the wild cherries that my mother warned
were poisonous), we ate and picked and ate and . . .
and ran out of ripe blackberries long before
even one tub was full.

And we walked slowly back up the hill
(into the sunset, into the fragrances of
barbecued chicken and citronella candles,
into the colors of Kool-Aid, and parsley
and paprika on potato salad), and we washed
the summer dust from our measly pint with
the garden hose, and offered them to mom,
who wrinkled her nose and unceremoniously
dumped them into the churn.

It was then that I made one of the great
discoveries of my young and very sensual life:
blackberries aren't really black, they're
deep purple; and they make home-made ice cream
just about the sexiest thing a sun-burned kid
can put in his mouth this side of hot, ripe
peaches, purloined from a neighbor's tree.

Childhood is a wonderful resource for poetry. It's dissolved in memory, so a dogged slavery to facts is unlikely to smother the poetic spirit. And it's filled with a prelapsarian sense of freedom and innocence.

Long before the present era of "helicopter parents," where both disapproval and parents are ubiquitous, it was ultimately permissive and sensual, without the slightest hint of sin. And for me, the most sensual season in childhood was always summer: nearly naked, barefoot, toasted dark brown, sunrise to sunset spent with gangs of kids pursuing every possible curiosity with guileless hearts. And cousins; there's something especially conspiratorial about cousins. It's only later that we realized that the adults were just trying to get rid of us, or that some of the things we did as children wouldn't be overlooked if we repeated them as adults. But that didn't matter then.

"Blackberries" is a sense poem. All five senses are given their due—and a couple of others: innocence and experience, to boot. In the "wrap up," I just had to toss St. Augustine a child's forgiveness for stealing those famous pears with his friends. It has been eating at him for about sixteen hundred years now and I think his instincts have been telling him all along that it was no big deal. I just wanted to confirm those instincts for him, child to child.

Diana Durham

SOMETHING ALMOST THE SAME

language is like a net, fine as fine grey
rain threading grey skies, wooded water ways
of the Whiskeag Creek's wide tributary
where over and over the rain lines say

something almost the same, just in case this
can be caught, or glimpsed intermittently
slipping along the trail, in a phrase
that captures miles, years of territory

it will stretch out as far as thought will go—
a mesh of lichen blooms, small pink moss lace
patterning the granite—it might just know
all this, it might just reach as far as space

it might just keep saying endless, endless
the rain on a grey creek, the spread of trees

> *Whiskeag Creek Trail, Kennebec Estuary Land Trust by Whiskeag Creek,*
> *tributary to the Kennebec River, near Bath, Maine*

We were visiting Bath in Maine and took a walk through a newly made trail by the Kennebec Estuary Land Trust that went up along the Whiskeag Creek. It was raining. Something about the rain on the water, and the unexpected wide expanse of land and water that could be glimpsed into the distance got me in touch with that extraordinary quality of North America, which perhaps as an Englishwoman, I am more susceptible to than those born and bred here—the sense of unending space, land, water, emptiness, bounty, grace, the vastness, the minuteness of scale—and instead this time of feeling slightly overwhelmed by it, I felt excitement, gratitude, wonder, and at the same time, a line came to me about language being a net, and somehow the wonder of it being able to continuously stretch out with our thought into this endlessness, the infinite universe.

Becky Dennison Sakellariou

SOME PRINCIPLE OF BEING*

For Stanley Kunitz

Come, quiet on your feet,
the path is lined with lavender
and yellow sweet pea.

Lean
over a bud, slip your ring finger under it,
stroke it with your thumb.

Examine the folds, the shell, the possibilities
of beauty and loneliness
and of you, still here.

You know that you are going.
Your voice cradles the lilac buds,
lifting their eyes one by one.

Words are not written
on this broken grass
bent from your feet, and mine;

wild yellow mustard
takes over the field beyond, no shame,
just a tiny bitter leaf.

And the wind bends the blossom
toward the impossible
blue sides of leaves.

You have known light
and color, the teal of the clippers,
the thin rust of dead leaves

keeping the earth musty
for the unlikely event
of another season.

The silver white mica
of the night sky slides
toward the cavern of all bodies.

*from "The Layers" by Stanley Kunitz

When I found the book, *Stanley Kunitz: A Life in Poetry and Gardens*, I was riveted by the cover photograph of the poet bent over studying something in his garden. I loved the tender, sweet attention and the deep, steady human spirit the photograph expressed. I spent a long time savoring the words, the poems, the photos, the interview, the essays, and I wanted to put this feeling, this integrity, this humility into a poem for Kunitz. I had never met him, so I wanted to know him a little, to follow him through the garden and imagine where he paused and what he might be thinking. I wanted to touch his mortality.

Deborah Brown

THE HUMAN HALF

Half-baked, my father used to say, meaning
that I was half in a state of nature, not yet
abashed into civilized form by parents
and other elders, the yeast still rising.
I'm consumed by who is cooked and who is not.
I see traces of wildness in our half-built house
and in the fond eye of a friend, the raw gleam
of a machete. It begins with the sperm's wild dash
to the egg. There's a half that's whole
in most of us, like members of a family,
one rich one poor, or the halves of this house—
the now and the hereafter, the part that loves,
the part that does not. Raw house, always half-built.
Raw human. Still half-baked. One hand
in the oven, the other half out the kitchen
door into the storm. If I could flee. Or bake.
But think of not having a home. There are
the homeless and those who do not have a homeland,
and the rest of us—homed, but only half-homed,
the wind whistling in from the shed and past us.

This poem, "The Human Half," began when I remembered an expression of
my father's. He used to call me, my ideas, anything he didn't agree with, really,
"half-baked." I began to think about that. I am also acutely aware of living in a
house that for the last ten years or so has been half-built. And then I remem-
bered reading, probably in a long-ago anthropology class, about Claude-Levi
Strauss's use of the terms "raw" and "cooked" to describe different types of
cultures. I believe I googled Levi Strauss to check on those words. I had fun
playing around with these three ideas, until they turned somber on me, as my
writing tends to do.

Carol Westberg

TYRANNY OF DREAMS

I don't mean to compete
over whose child suffers more,

yours bleeding hope away each month
or mine signed up for her first

shock treatment. The moon's impassive
over all our children's dreams.

As a mother I know fear
wraps its hands around the throat.

A phone call can turn the night air to ice.
Today a fire burns in the woodstove

for real, and Garrison Keillor is joking
on the radio about selective

serotonin reuptake inhibitors.
I doubt his son ever took up a razor

and sliced line by line into his thigh
to silence voices clamoring inside himself.

But what do I know of his son,
our daughters? They all must strive

to rise each day and find
two comfortable shoes to slip into.

I've grown wary of the tyranny of dreams.
Just now I mean to pad downstairs

for tea and toast that I'll spread thick
with your wild plum jam.

➣

It's rare for a poem to come to me in one sitting like this one. The triggering incident was listening to Garrison Keillor joke about SSRI's on his radio show, thinking about the real people these drugs save. I'm especially grateful for friends who've shared hopes and fears for our daughters living with challenges of mental and physical health. May we honor their dreams.

Nancy Lagomarsino

WE NEED THE BODIES

Bodies from TWA Flight 800 lost in the sea, bodies from the
ValuJet crash sucked below the surface of the Everglades, never to
be reclaimed, never to receive a parting kiss. Bereft families hang
suspended between death and grief.

Since these tragedies, I've heard people say they don't understand why
the families want the bodies back so much. "The spirit has departed,"
they insist. "It's just a body."

Just a body. But the body has a spirit, too, the same spirit that inhabits
seashells, iridescent nests shining in the water's branches with the
memory of once-held life. Much of my father's spirit has flowed into
his body, to fill the hollows left by disease. I touch him often, for solace,
seeming to touch spirit more than flesh.

Of course, we need the bodies. At death, the body's spirit departs
slowly, having much to occupy it. We can gather the body in our arms
and say, Good-bye, I love you. Each touch is a thought to the body's
spirit. The impatient soul hurries ahead, turning to wait for the body's
spirit to catch up, because the soul misses the body, though the two
often have been at odds. The soul throws a comforting arm around
the body's spirit, and they go forward together, the body's spirit with a
dragging step, the soul like quicksilver.

We need the bodies.

"We need the bodies" appears in *Light from an Eclipse* midway through my dad's
journey into Alzheimer's disease. At that point, his deterioration had proceeded
enough to make my visits to Cape Cod exceedingly stressful. I would return to
New Hampshire with doubts about whether I'd managed to rise to the occasion
and fears about what the future would ask of us. Writing was my main therapy,
along with a support group for those affected by the disease. This is one of my
favorite poems from the book, because it sprung fully formed, requiring almost
no revision. The trigger was hearing someone say she didn't understand why
people want the bodies back so much. It made me mad, because my dad's brain
was vanishing; the poem was my response.

Sylva Boyadjian-Haddad

GOD'S SCHEDULE

We keep God occupied with our routines,
rituals of offerings, hymns, incense, intense
prayers, genuflections and such. We build

cathedrals that shiver with centuries
of hypocrisy and ignorance, at times
even hope and repentance and sacrifice

so that we could continue our merry
carnage without interference.

I like poetry to be concise, its language as spare as it possibly can be and still
mean something. Perhaps even surprise us. Resonate. Everything has the power
to inspire, hence one has to consciously immerse oneself in this world with-
out forgetting the past, since the past informs and shapes the present. Above
all else, one has to open oneself up and be vulnerable, while allowing oneself
ample time to think, contemplate and wait. After a while a poem will form itself.
Then the actual work—the crafting—begins, which for me includes a merciless
elimination of what I deem superfluous. "God's Schedule" is a reflection on
hypocrisy (here I must confess that I am a news junkie) and the outcome of the
process described above.

Gordon Lang

DOS EQUIS

When you drop your ex off at the clinic on North Rampart,
blow the Quarter: hang a left on St. Bernard,
you'll be on I-10 in a twinkle, so blink and pull the visor down—
the rising sun is blinding as you slide out toward Slidell,
past every Picayune post office in Mississippi.
Tip your hat to Hattiesburg, shoot Birmingham a bye-bye, then
chug on up to Chattanooga—you'll be knocking outside Knoxville
by nightfall. That's when things get hairy, around Marion:

you're bleary, you shouldn't really still be driving but
you bull on into Bluefield after spiraling down through tunnel
after tunnel and you're so dizzy when you finally churn
into the back lot of some Dunkins you can't recall blowing up
the donut pillow or the crawl into the back seat
when the trooper blasts his flashlight, moves you on.
Sun-up along the Alleghenies whips your ridge-run
to a frothy simmer, then ladles you down into a morning porringer,

Morgantown. In a café there, towering over a butcher block,
dark hair cocked to one side, leans your double ex,
the one before last, cleaver in hand, shaving the fruit
from shaft after shaft of corn. The new meat, some grad student
stewing in back, won't fit in your poor chowder head: you are cut
so thoroughly loose you could cry and do, but only later, swimming
with them and a beer, far out into the man-made lake,
which seems bottomless, but for the strip mine it hides below.

In those brief, lucky seasons when I get to teach creative writing, I try to write
along with my students and respond to the same prompts they do. I also have
my students do at least as much reading as they do writing. To get my students
to write poems that have movement to them, I asked them to write about phys-
ically going from one place to another. "Dos Equis" came from a unit I call

"road poems." We prepared for this by reading things such as Raymond Carver's "Waiting," Kurt Brown's "Road Trip," and George Bradley's "Leaving Kansas City." I told them, "Pick a road, any road; follow it to the next intersection or association or crossing animal; pick up that trail and follow it to the next crossing, and again and again until you reach some destination."

Andrew Booth

THE SPECIFICS

Neil Patrick Harris & David Burtke: Cover, *Out Magazine,* January 2012

Because one will stand
& straighten the tie of one he loves.
Because he will press his head to theirs
smelling of aftershave & feel his nose
beneath their mouth & feel his hands
against their shirt.
Because of gentleness,
coyness,
the asymmetrical
gesture before embrace.
Because of the grip
of their hands, the quiet
seriousness of their faces.
Because the world exists also for them
just as the hedge & leaf pulled
into semi-focus at their chins.
Because it is good to touch; because
there is no evil in love's manufacture
poised before a breath in the garden.
The distance between hate & empathy
is attention.

I wrote "The Specifics" in winter, on one of those days when everything and everyone seems rotten. The weather was terrible. The Republican debates were getting full coverage on the radio and hatred seemed to be in full swing—anti-gay, anti-women, minorities, foreign relations, education, future, past—you name it. So I was aimlessly surfing the web, trying to shake the funk off, and found where someone had posted this picture of Neil Patrick Harris and David Burtke kind of pressed together in a garden. Not erotic, mind you, but certainly posed with romantic intention. It struck me. I broke down at my desk and started weeping, and out came the poem. But it came strangely, with all the fear and pain and excitement of those first poems you write, the awful ones, when you're sixteen, seventeen, and all strung out on puberty. I'm still not certain exactly how it comes across, but the process of writing it reminded me why I started this endeavor in the first place.

J. Kates

WORDS

after V. S. Rabenchuk

I write. I command. The word is an animal
to the truth—sometimes a flower or stone
or star, you say?—no, always a beast, and one
it's up to each of us to bring to heel.

I track words through their laughter and their tears.
I crack my whip and order them: Be divine!
Love one another! They snarl and pace the line
and ravage a carrion meal when it appears.

I watch them fly in chevrons overhead,
looking for quiet waters. I set out
decoys to bring them close enough to shoot.
After the first, even the last has fled.

I lie in wait among the quiet reeds
for a word to swallow the hook, come flashing up
like sunrise and flap gasping in the scupper.
Dying, the scales turn gray; a small mouth bleeds.

"Words" began as a translation from a language (Ukrainian) I am able to read
only through a glass darkly. It took on a life of its own at about the same time
I recognized my own incompetence to make proper English sense of the origi-
nal. The animal schematics I devised (earth, air, water) led inevitably to the last
stanza, which alludes to an afternoon I spent fishing on the Yuzhny Bug River
with the Ukrainian poet whose own poem had started these "Words."

Janet Sylvester

SEA SMOKE

Frost on a window, indistinguishable from roses
knotted into a curtain, burning
        as blue dawn drains into it
        from the backyard apple, its parabola
of ruddy spheres
what's left of summer. Across the fence, a red boat's dry docked,
buttoned against snow
        that won't arrive until later.
        Warming your hands
at a cup of coffee
in the kitchen, you send your wish into the hemlocks, and
beyond them, to the bridge
        that takes you away, commuting days.
        You want to root here,
into the water's going
and coming, to be home, to be home, in this old place
long skirts hurried
        through to the small barn
        a Mexican restaurant worker rents
now. Instead, you layer sweaters,
walk out to scrape ice from the car, coughing, like luck, into drive.
Past the Square that plows
        have already heaped into drifts,
        you slide onto the bridge
and—how can it be worded—the braiding tensions of the current,
the light the world flows inside,
have turned to precious metals.
        Every register of platinum
        and rose gold issues into.
the frigid channel, coaxed
by sun into thermal plumes, bright steam cooling to droplets bent
by air into pyramids—
        dozens of them—
        seemingly still. You

stop, idling for minutes
to let the bridge raise, then drop; the day's first fruit, a form of fog
exhaled by water,

       already gone, as
       the future accumulates

in the rear-view mirror: an apple tree,
dirt-brown, disappearing into the vanished chapel of its leaves.

Before moving to Portsmouth, New Hampshire, in 2008, I lived in Kittery, Maine, for a year and commuted to Boston for work. I crossed the now missing Memorial Bridge countless times.

Stopped on the bridge one frigid February day, I looked to my left at the harbor and saw what appeared to be a visual artist's rendering of a spiritual state: water, lit with dozens of slightly tilted triangles made of steam in ineffable shades of silver, copper, pink, and pale blue under the early-morning sun. The vision was riveting, and then traffic was given the signal to move forward. I discovered that the phenomenon is called sea smoke. It's the heart of the poem, beating in that sinuous collocation of canals, river, and harbor islands, a tidal place.

Living in Kittery, and then Portsmouth, the daily motion of the water, visible or invisible, informed who I was. I can still feel it. When I began to work on the poem, layered as most of my poems are, this heart beat among other images of the place the water moved through—its history, its present vivid as the back-yard's old apple tree. I was home; I wasn't home yet. Little did I know. When the tide recently returned me to New Hampshire, I relearned its truth.

Ala Khaki

CONUNDRUM

Just over the edge of reason,
near the brink of madness,
lies love,
enthralling, exuberant,
splendid, mysterious, and dangerous—
       a space-time warp
       infused with the spirit of
       winged stallions
       and wounded mares.

For the soul who dares
       to explore
       awaits a whirlwind of emotions
       unlike anything
       experienced before—
          from the rush of ecstasy
             on the flight
                to the summit of wholeness,
          to the crush of exile
             on the fall
                to the arctic of loneliness
          and everything in between.

Nothing is safe
and everything is possible
between two breaths.

Enter at your peril
and live
as the Sun,
as the Sea.

Or don't
and never know
what it means
to be.

Following a painful divorce in 2002, I went through a period of cynicism and disillusionment about love. A few attempts at breaking new ground only amplified these sentiments. A short-lived romance inspired "Conundrum." Alas, it too was a mirage. I probably would have destroyed the poem had it not been for the wonderful soul which has completed mine since 2008.

Barbara Bald

NEVERLAND

Let's pretend, she said to her friend
running down the hill in the opposite direction.
Let's pretend, she said to the sky, to the air,
to the field around her.

Arms held high, as if performing for God,
she danced in a white long-sleeved blouse
and a plaid skirt over black knee-highs.

Blond hair blowing in fall breezes,
her hips gyrated to the beat in her head,
like Tinker Bell savoring Never-Never-Land.

Waving like one of those lilies of the field
that lives carefree under divine protection,
she touched tall grasses,
holding deep conversations with them.

Watched from a distance,
she did not hide in embarrassment—rather,
she heightened the pitch of her twirling
with the air of a princess pleasing her subjects.

How long would it take for her to lose
that spark of self-absorption,
that feeling that she was enough?

Perhaps some teacher would criticize
her crayoned elephant,
a parent would tell her kissing donkeys
wasn't proper or friends wouldn't choose her
for their softball team?

When would she become self-conscious
or ashamed, pulling in like a threatened turtle?
How old a woman would she have to be
to start talking to grasses again?

At a Native American celebration, I was privileged to witness a little girl and her friend playing in a field. Her freedom from self-consciousness, her total self-acceptance and complete immersion in what the moment offered mesmerized me. Then, I slipped into regret—thinking about all the judgments laid upon myself and others as we grew up. I began postulating if and when that might happen to her. Watching some of that "freedom from" and "freedom to" re-emerge in myself as I age, I ended the poem questioning when that return to innocence might happen for her and, ultimately, all of us.

Bill Burtis

CHASE

For Martine

One day, leaving the park
by the ocean beach, I looked
up from installing your sister
in her car seat, to see you
running toward the park gate,
arms outstretched, after a car
that looked like ours.

I knew everything at once—
What you believed, how your spirit
would be bowed, how you
were staggered by your tears.

Today, a boy that small, three perhaps,
still young enough that his intention to run
outdistances the capacity of his legs
to carry him at such speeds—
in jeans and a bright green sweatshirt
is chasing pigeons in the park
endlessly turning
to find a new pigeon.

Remarkably, they do not fly
but run on their little legs
ahead of him as if understanding
perfectly this child's game.
He runs and runs, turning
to one pigeon after another.
There is nothing else in his world.

Instinctively I scan the park and eventually
find him, the grandfather in this case, wisely,
like a grandfather, keeping his distance, giving
this boy his rein, his world.

→

A lot of my poetry exorcises demons. This one, in particular, looks at my feelings of failure as a father—feelings I know I share with many fathers—but in an oblique way, which I prefer to stabbing myself in the head. I'm particularly fond of this poem because I conceived the last three stanzas almost as they are on my cell phone, as a message on my home answering machine. Martine is my eldest daughter.

Deming Holleran

INTO THE MIST

Fog shawls the silent river
and the islands' shoulders, and a loon call
lingers on the early morning light.
My mother lies in the cool bedroom air
of her house of fifty summers.
She is nearly eighty-eight, and weary,
opening her clouded eyes on one more day.
I see her head propped on pillows, faded
nightgown collar lace barely thinner
than the folds of skin it covers. We
are alone, and she asks *where am I?*
I cannot answer. I do not really know.
Her voice, my mother's voice, is high,
as hollow as the loon's. She leans
toward me, stretching hands like
sparrow talons searching for a perch.
My hands meet hers, and I am pulled down,
down into the mist, into the pillowed
cloudbank and the withered scent of her,
and I answer from the only place
that matters now, *you are with me.*

"Into the Mist" was written during the time my mother was fast sinking into
the emotional and physical ravages of dementia and old age. Her surroundings
were no longer familiar to her, and I found some solace in writing this "found"
poem.

Biographies

RICK AGRAN lives in Montpelier, Vermont. He teaches writing, literature, humanities and photojournalism at Johnson State College. Rick wrote *Pumpkin Shivaree*, a children's picture book, and a collection of poems, *Crow Milk*. He co-edited *Under the Legislature of Stars: 62 New Hampshire Poets* which included thirty-three poets from the Poet Showcase. In small rural schools, Rick teaches poetry and arts integration for Vermont and New Hampshire Arts Councils and the Children's Literacy Foundation. Garrison Keillor has read his poems on "The Writers' Almanac" and anthologized them in *Great Poems, American Places*. Visit www.crowmilk.org.

LIZ AHL is the author of *Talking About the Weather* (Seven Kitchens Press, 2012), *Luck* (Pecan Grove Press, 2010), and *A Thirst That's Partly Mine*. Her poems have appeared in many literary journals and some have received Pushcart Prize nominations. Her work has also been included in several anthologies, including *This Assignment is So Gay: LGBTIQ Poets on the Art of Teaching* (Sibling Rivalry Press, 2013), and *Mischief, Caprice, and Other Poetic Strategies* (Red Hen Press, 2004). She has been awarded residencies at Playa, Jentel, the Kimmel Harding Nelson Center for the Arts, and The Vermont Studio Center. She teaches at Plymouth State University in Plymouth, New Hampshire.

JOHN-MICHAEL ALBERT (Mike) is the editor of *The Poets' Guide to New Hampshire* (Poetry Society of New Hampshire, 2008 and 2010), a travel guide to the state containing 400 poems by 300 poets from the last two centuries. His most recent books of poetry are *The Bird Catcher: New and Selected Poems* (Moon Pie Press, 2012) and *Cardamom Cravings, Notes for an Autobiography* (Sargent Press, 2012). Mike is also the author of a collection of essays on modern poetry, *The Light and Air of Our Work* (Marble Kite, 2013). He is the eighth Portsmouth Poet Laureate (2011–2013). John-Michael.Albert@comcast.net

BARBARA BALD is a retired teacher, educational consultant and freelance writer. Her poems have been published in a variety of anthologies: *The Other Side of Sorrow*, the 2008 and 2010 *Poets' Guide to New Hampshire*, *For Loving Precious Beast*, *Sun and Sand*, *Tic Toc*, and many others. They have appeared in several literary journals including *The Northern New England Review*, *Avocet*, and *Off the Coast*. Her work has been recognized in both national and local contests. She has a chapbook called *Running on Empty* and a full-length book called *Drive-Through Window*. www.barbarabald.com

L. R. BERGER'S collection of poems, *The Unexpected Aviary*, received the 2003 Jane Kenyon Award for Outstanding Book of Poetry. She's been the grateful recipient of fellowships and support from the National Endowment for the Arts, the PEN New England Discovery Award, the New Hampshire State Council on the Arts, the MacDowell Colony, the Blue Mountain Center, Wellspring and The American Academy in Rome. With Kamal Boullatta, she assisted in the translation from the Arabic of "Beginnings" by Adonis (Pyramid Atlantic Press). For fifteen years she was inspired by her creative writing students at the University of Massachusetts/Boston. She lives and writes within earshot of the Contoocook River.

PAM BERNARD, a poet, painter, editor, and adjunct professor, received her MFA in Creative Writing from the Graduate Program for Writers at Warren Wilson College, and her BA from Harvard University in History of Art. Her awards include a National Endowment for the Arts Fellowship in Poetry, two Massachusetts Cultural Council Fellowships, the Grolier Prize in Poetry, and a MacDowell Fellowship. She has published three full-length collections of poetry and a novel in verse, *Esther*, published by CavanKerry Press. Ms. Bernard lives in Walpole, New Hampshire, and teaches writing at New Hampshire Institute of Art and Franklin Pierce University.

ANNA BIRCH grew up in Hollis New Hampshire, and spent many years on the New Hampshire seacoast before returning to Hollis in 2010 to live in her family's ancestral multi-generational home. She is an artist and printmaker, running Queen Oscar Designs, and teaches art classes to kids and adults. She graduated from the Univeristy of New Hampshire and has been a member of Portsmouth's City Hall Poets since 1995. She continues to write poetry and attends workshops and conferences, living and working in Hollis with her husband, artist Christopher Volpe, and their son Max.

ANDREW BOOTH is a recent graduate of the University of New Hampshire's MFA program in poetry and a current server/busser/baby juggler/all-around-yes-man in Portsmouth's breakfast business. He's trying to learn to play golf (i.e. hit a golf ball) and working on several translations from Paul Eluard and Tristan Tzara between more elaborate chapbook projects. He lives on the Great Bay and considers all the wildlife his pets.

LISA BOURBEAU shares a hillside in Francestown with an aging greyhound and four wild horses. Her poetry and criticism have appeared in numerous online and print journals, including *webdelsol, Talisman: A Literary Journal*, and *Ploughshares*, and she is the author of *Cuttings from the Garden of Little Fears*. She is currently working on a translation of selected poems of the Turkish poet Lâle Müldür.

SYLVA BOYADJIAN-HADDAD, Professor of English and Comparative Literature, Emerita, is a poet, writer, and translator. She is the founder and editor-in-chief of *Entelechy International: A Journal of Contemporary Ideas*. Her work has appeared in numerous literary journals, magazines, and anthologies. She has been nominated several times for a Pushcart Prize. *Salt*, her collection of poems released by Finishing Line Press in 2011, was the recipient for the third Honorable Mention for the New Women's Voices Prize in 2010. Currently she is finishing a new collection of poetry and doing research for a novel.

DEBORAH BROWN'S book of poems, *Walking the Dog's Shadow*, was the 2010 winner of the A. J. Poulin Jr. Award from BOA Editions, as well as the 2011 winner of the NHLA Award for Outstanding Book of Poetry. The title poem won a Pushcart Prize in 2013. Brown is a translator, with Richard Jackson and Susan Thomas, of *Last Voyage: Selected Poems of Giovanni Pascoli* (Red Hen Press, 2010) and an editor, with Maxine Kumin and Annie Finch, of *Lofty Dogmas: Poets on Poetics* (University of Arkansas Press, 2005) Her poems have appeared in *Margie, Rattle, The Mississippi Review* and others. Brown is a professor of English at the University of New Hampshire in Manchester where she won an award for Excellence in Teaching.

PRISCILLA BURLINGHAM, a graduate of the Museum of Fine Arts School in Boston, was first encouraged to write poetry while on painting fellowships at Ragdale and Yaddo. In the mid-nineties, poetry took over as her major medium. She has since sparked poetry readings in North Country libraries and has gathered talent from all over New England to read monthly next to city, state and United States poets laureate at the Moultonborough Public Library. She writes almost without pause in her studio in the Lakes Region. The few poems that have appeared in anthologies are from her 2010 book, *A Finer Reach*.

DON BURNESS was born in Hartford, Connecticut in 1941. He has lived in eight countries, traveled in more than eighty, and speaks seven languages. He is the author of twenty-three books including eleven collections of poetry. His twelfth book, *Tombstones* (Twenty-three Books), was published in 2010. He is the American correspondent to *Odissea* (Milan, Italy), a paper devoted to cultural and social issues. An exhibit of his paintings, "Poetry and Painting," was held from September to October, 2009 at the Hancock, New Hampshire Library. He has been given the title Ojemba Enweilo (traveler who makes no enemy) by his friend, the Nigerian writer Chinua Achebe.

BILL BURTIS is a Boston native who became interested in poetry while studying with James Crenner at Hobart College in Geneva, New York. He attended the Iowa Writers Workshop from 1971 to 1973 where he studied with Marvin Bell, Albert Goldbarth, Anselm Hollo, Norman Dubie, and his adviser, Donald Justice. He moved to New Hampshire in 1975 and taught writing in a number of venues. He has published poems in several literary journals including *The Paris Review*, *Chelsea*, and *Sou'wester*, and in a chapbook, *Villains*, (L'Epervier Press, 1976, out of print). He is currently working on three manuscripts of poems at his home in Stratham, New Hampshire, where he writes and lives with the poet Nancy Jean Hill, one cat and one dog.

W. E. BUTTS authored ten poetry collections, including *Cathedral of Nervous Horses* (Hobblebush Books, 2012) and *Sunday Evening at the Stardust Café*, the winner of the 2006 Iowa Source Poetry Book Prize. His poems appeared in many journals such as *Atlantic Review*, *Cimarron Review*, *Mid-American Review*, *Poetry East*, and in many anthologies. Butts was the recipient of two Pushcart Prize nominations and a Massachusetts Artist Foundation Award. He taught in the BFA in Creative Writing Program at Goddard College and was the New Hampshire Poet Laureate from 2009 until his death in 2013. His final book of poems, *Story & Luck* was published by Adastra Press in 2015.

MARTHA CARLSON-BRADLEY is the author of *Sea Called Fruitfulness* (WordTech Editions, 2013), *If I Take You Here* (Adastra, 2011), *Season We Can't Resist* (WordTech Editions, 2007), *Beast at the Hearth* (Adastra, 2005), and *Nest Full of Cries* (Adastra, 2000). Her poems have appeared in many literary magazines, including *New England Review*, *LA Review*, *Salamander*, and *Zone 3*, and in anthologies, such as *The Poets' Grimm* (Story Line Press, 2003). Her awards include fellowships from the American Antiquarian Society and the New Hampshire State Council on the Arts. She lives in Hillsborough, New Hampshire, near Fox State Forest.

EWA CHRUSCIEL has two books in English, *Contraband of Hoopoe* (Omnidawn Press, 2014) and *Strata* (Emergency Press, 2011) and two books in Polish: *Furkot* and *Sopilki*. Her poems were featured in *Jubilat*,

Boston Review, Colorado Review, Lana Turner, Spoon River Review, Aufgabe, among others. She has translated Jack London, Joseph Conrad, I.B. Singer as well as Jorie Graham, Lyn Hejinian, Cole Swensen and other American poets into Polish. She is an associate professor at Colby-Sawyer College. www.echrusciel.net.

MARNIE COBBS works as a bookbinder, conserving rare books and whatever else comes her way, like third-generation cookbooks. She has always written poems and likes to paint as well, and started The Uphill House in 1998 to create her own books and cards.

CHRISTINA N. Cook is the author of *Lake Effect* (Finishing Line Press, 2012), winner of the Jean Pedrick Chapbook Prize. Her work has appeared in journals such as *New Ohio Review, Crab Orchard Review, Hayden's Ferry Review*, and *Dos Passos Review*. A graduate of Vermont College of Fine Arts, Christina is also an essayist, book critic, and translator. She works as a writer in the University of Pennsylvania's Office of Communications.

SCOTT COYKENDALL teaches professional writing classes at Plymouth State University where he is a member of the Communication and Media Studies Department. With his wife and two daughters, along with various cats, dogs, fish, and chickens, he lives and writes in Plymouth, New Hampshire.

ROBERT W. CRAWFORD has published two books of poetry, *The Empty Chair* (2011 Richard Wilbur Award), and *Too Much Explanation Can Ruin a Man*. His sonnets have twice won the Howard Nemerov Sonnet Award. His poems have appeared in many national journals including *The Formalist, First Things, Dark Horse, The Raintown Review, The Lyric, Measure, Light* and *Forbes*. Currently, he is the director of the Frost Farm Poetry Conference, and is the JV head / assistant head football coach at Pelham High School. He lives in Chester, New Hampshire, with his wife, the poet Midge Goldberg.

MARK DECARTERET'S work has appeared in the anthologies *American Poetry: The Next Generation* (Carnegie Mellon Press), *Place of Passage: Contemporary Catholic Poetry* (Story Line Press), *Thus Spake the Corpse: An Exquisite Corpse Reader* (Black Sparrow Press) and *Under the Legislature of Stars—62 New Hampshire Poets* (Oyster River Press) which he also co-edited. From 2009 to 2011 he was the Poet Laureate of Portsmouth, New Hampshire. You can check out his Postcard Project at pplp.org.

MAGGIE DIETZ is the author of *Perennial Fall*, which won New Hampshire's 2007 Jane Kenyon Award for Outstanding Book of Poetry, and *That Kind of Happy* (both from University of Chicago Press). For many years she directed the Favorite Poem Project and is coeditor, with Robert Pinsky, of three anthologies related to the project: *Americans' Favorite Poems*, *Poems to Read*, and *An Invitation to Poetry* (all W. W. Norton & Co.). She teaches at the University of Massachusetts Lowell.

MARTHA ANDREWS DONOVAN, author of the chapbook *Dress Her in Silk* (Finishing Line Press, 2009), is a writer, teacher, and workshop leader. Her essay "Dangerous Archaeology: A Daughter's Search for Her Mother (and Others)" (with photographer Autumn E. Monsees) was named a "Notable Essay" by *The Best American Essays 2013*. Her writing explores the intersections between memory, image, and narrative, and the ways in which the things we unearth—photographs, artifacts, ephemera, and other fragmentary evidence—can help narrate a life. She is musing at: *One Writer's Excavation: Narrating a Life, Piece by Piece* (https://madonovan.wordpress.com)

WILLIAM DORESKI lives in Peterborough, New Hampshire, and teaches at Keene State College. His most recent book of poetry is *The Suburbs of Atlantis* (2013). He has published three critical studies, including *Robert Lowell's Shifting Colors*. His essays, poetry, fiction, and reviews have appeared in many journals.

JAMES DUFFY lives in Keene, New Hampshire. He holds an MFA in Writing from Vermont College. His poetry has appeared in *Ploughshares*, *MUSE*, *Contemporary Review*, *Aurora*, and *Crying Sky: Poetry and Conversation*. His poem, "Prayer," was included in the anthology *Under the Legislature of Stars: 62 New Hampshire Poets*.

ROBERT DUNN grew up in Meredith and attended the University of New Hampshire where he became an activist for a number of causes. He went on to work in the Civil Rights Movement, registering African-Americans to vote in the South, and to protest the Vietnam War. For most of his adult life, he lived in Portsmouth, New Hampshire, where he sold his handmade books of poems on the street for a penny. From 1999 to 2001, he served as the Poet Laureate of Portsmouth. During this time, he sponsored a project to place poetry in public places around the city, including the walls of the parking garage where the poems he helped choose remain visible. He died in 2008.

DIANA DURHAM is the author of three poetry collections, including *Between Two Worlds* (Chrysalis Press, UK) and *To the End of the Night* (Northwoods Press, Maine); the nonfiction *The Return of King Arthur* (Tarcher/ Penguin) and a debut novel *The Curve of the Land* (Skylight Press). Her poetry has been featured in numerous journals and anthologies in the United Kingdom and the United States. Durham was a member of the London poetry performance group Angels of Fire. In New Hampshire she founded "3 Voices" with Maren Tirabassi and Rebecca Rule. She holds a BA in English Literature from University College, London.

LINDA DYER writes both poetry and prose. Her work has appeared in literary journals such as *Birmingham Poetry Review*, *Poet Lore*, *Slant* and *Exit 13*, anthologies including *The Blueline Anthology*, *Heartbeat of New England* and *Where the Mountain Stands Alone*, online publications such as *Redux* and *Brevity* as well as newspapers, including the *New York Times* and the *Christian Science Monitor*. She lives in Amherst, New Hampshire.

JANE EKLUND'S poems have been published in journals, including the *Georgia Review*, *The Sun*, and the *Massachusetts Review*. She has received fellowships from the Iowa and New Hampshire state arts councils for poetry and the Astraea Foundation for fiction, and has been granted residencies at Blue Mountain Center and Virginia Center for the Creative Arts. A graduate of Colby College and the University of Iowa Writers' Workshop, she lives in Hancock and works as the alumni magazine editor at Keene State College.

NEIL ENGLISH is a performance poet. His work has been published in the anthologies *Portsmouth Unabridged: New Poems for an Old City*, *Entelechy International: A Journal of Contemporary Ideas*, *The Other Side of Sorrow* and both the 2008 and the 2010 *Poets' Guide to New Hampshire*. A former Vice President of the Poetry Society of New Hampshire, he has recited his work at poetry venues throughout New England, the Goffstown Women's Prison and New Hampshire schools from the elementary grades through the university level. He lives in Epsom, New Hampshire.

KATHLEEN FAGLEY teaches creative writing at Keene State College. Her poetry has appeared in *The Comstock Review*, *Cutthroat*, *Memoir Journal*, *The Stillwater Review*, *Connotation Press: An Online Artifact*, and others. Finishing Line Press published her chapbook, *How You Came to Me* in July 2012. Her critical essay on Jean Valentine's poetry was included with twenty-five other poets in a 2012 publication of the University of Michigan titled: *Jean Valentine: This-World Company* edited by Kazim Ali and John Hoppenthaler.

PATRICIA FARGNOLI, the New Hampshire Poet Laureate from 2006 to 2009, has published four award-winning books of poetry and three chapbooks. Her newest publication, *Winter* (Hobblebush Books, 2013) was volume VI in the Hobblebush Granite State Poetry Series. Her book, *Then, Something* (Tupelo Press, 2009) won the *ForeWord Magazine* Silver Poetry Book Award, The Shelia Mooton Book Award, an Honorable Mention in the Eric Hoffer Book Awards and was a finalist for the 2011 New Hampshire Literary Awards. A Macdowell Fellow, she's published over 300 poems in anthologies and literary journals such as *Ploughshares, Mid-American Review, Massachusetts Review* and others. She's a retired psychotherapist.

KELLY M. FLYNN studied poetry as an undergraduate at Harvard with Seamus Heaney and Helen Vendler, and received her MFA in poetry at the Iowa Writers' Workshop, where she studied with Jorie Graham, Jim Galvin, Mark Doty, and Marvin Bell. A native of Missouri, she currently teaches English at Phillips Exeter Academy in Exeter, New Hampshire, where she also directs theater and plays the organ and piano.

LAURA DAVIES FOLEY is the author of four poetry collections. *The Glass Tree* won the *ForeWord Magazine's* Book of the Year Award, Silver, and was a Finalist for the New Hampshire Writer's Project's Outstanding Book of Poetry. *Joy Street* won the the Bi-Writer's Award in Poetry. Her poems have appeared in many journals, including *Valparaiso Poetry Review, Inquiring Mind, Pulse Magazine, Poetry Nook, Lavender Review, The Mom Egg Review* and in the anthologies *In the Arms of Words: Poems for Disaster Relief* and *Weatherings*. She won *Harpur Palate's* Poetry Award and the Grand Prize for *Atlanta Review's* International Poetry Contest.

MARY SPOFFORD FRENCH was born on Thanksgiving Day in 1932, married her husband Jack in 1951, and was blessed with eight children. Through marriages they nearly doubled their "children" and were given seventeen grandchildren and nine great-grandchildren. She is a collector of family stories, memorabilia, and photos. At the University of New Hampshire she took a writing class with Charles Simic and later a weeklong workshop with Wes McNair. She belongs to the Yogurt Poets writing group.

JEFF FRIEDMAN has published six poetry collections, five with Carnegie Mellon University Press, including *Pretenders* (2014), *Working in Flour* (2011) and *Black Threads* (2008). His poems, mini stories and translations have appeared in many literary magazines, including *American Poetry Review, Poetry, New England Review, The Antioch Review, Poetry International, Hotel Amerika, Vestal Review, Flash Fiction Funny, Smokelong Quarterly, Prairie Schooner, 100-Word Story, Agni Online, Plume, Journal of Compressed Creative Arts,* and *The New Republic.* Dzvinia Orlowsky's and Jeff's translation of *Memorials* by Polish Poet Mieczslaw Jastrun was published by Lavender Ink/Dialogos in August 2014. He and Orlowsky were awarded an NEA Literature Translation Fellowship for 2016.

PAT FRISELLA, former president of the Poetry Society of New Hampshire, edited the anthology, *The Other Side of Sorrow: Poets Speak Out About Conflict, War and Peace* (Poetry Society of New Hampshire, 2006), which won the 2007 bronze prize from the Independent Book Awards. She is a board member of the nonprofit Art Esprit which has created large-scale public art installations in collaborations between visual artists and poets. Work is forthcoming in collaboration with Aldo Tambellini, Tontongi, Askia Touré and others. She lives in a small town on a tree farm with her husband and a menagerie of creatures great and small. She can be found on Facebook, Twitter and the web at www.patriciafrisella.com.

BILL GARVEY, formerly of Keene, New Hampshire, resides with his Canadian wife in Halifax, Nova Scotia. His poetry has been published or is forthcoming in several journals including *Margie, The Worcester Review, 5AM, Slant, Diner, Concho River Review, New York Quarterly,* and others. Finishing Line Press published his chapbook, *The Burden of Angels,* in 2007. Bill received his MFA from New England College in Henniker.

SHELLEY GIRDNER'S poems have been published in several journals, including most recently *Hunger Mountain* and *Painted Bride Quarterly,* as well as *The Indiana Review, Mid-American Review,* and others. She's been a featured poet in *The Aurorean,* a finalist for the Slappering Hol Chapbook Prize, and has been nominated for a Pushcart Prize in poetry. She teaches at the University of New Hampshire.

KATE GLEASON is the author of a full-length collection of poetry, *Measuring the Dark* (selected by Phillis Levin as the winner of the First Book Award at Zone 3 Press), and three chapbooks, most recently *Reading*

Darwin While My Father Dies (Anabiosis Press). Her work has appeared in *Best American Poetry*, *Verse Daily*, *Los Angeles Times Book Review*, *Alaska Quarterly Review*, *Rattle*, and elsewhere. A Pushcart Prize nominee, she has received writing fellowships from the NEA (in conjunction with the Ragdale Foundation artist colony), the Vermont Studio Center, and the New Hampshire State Council on the Arts. Formerly the editor of *Peregrine*, she teaches writing workshops and runs Writers Submit, a literary submitting and editing service.

BILL GLEED was born in Amesbury, Massachusetts and grew up in Haverhill, Massachusetts. He is a 1995 graduate of the master's creative writing program in poetry at the University of New Hampshire. He spent eleven summers as the manager of the Robert Frost Farm in Derry. While there, Bill co-founded the Hyla Brook Poets workshop and reading series. He has taught English and writing at several colleges and universities and has published poetry in the *Boston Globe*, *Concrete Wolf*, the *Houston Poetry Festival Anthology*, and others. He was poetry editor at the UNESCO award-winning website moondance.org and is currently a contributing editor and poetry editor for *Maelstrom*.

MIDGE GOLDBERG'S poems have appeared in *Measure*, *First Things*, *Appalachia*, and on Garrison Keillor's *A Writer's Almanac*, among others. Her manuscript *Snowman's Code* recently won the 2015 Richard Wilbur Poetry Award and will be published by University of Evansville Press. She has an MFA in Writing Poetry from the University of New Hampshire and taught poetry at Chester College of New England. She lives in Chester, New Hampshire.

DONALD HALL, former United States Poet Laureate, was born in Connecticut in 1928. He has published eighteen books of poems and numerous books of prose and children's books. He lives by himself on his family farm in Wilmot, New Hampshire. His most recent book, December 2014, was *Essays After Eighty*, and this December he will publish *The Selected Poems of Donald Hall*.

MARTHA DEBORAH HALL'S poems have appeared in numerous journals including *Bellowing Ark*, *Common Ground Review*, *Las Cruces*, *Tapestries*, and *The Poet's Touchstone*. She is the winner of the 2005 John and Miriam Morris Chapbook contest for her collection *Abandoned Gardens*. She was a semifinalist in both the 2007 Concrete Wolf Chapbook Contest and the 2010 Kathryn A. Morton Prize in Poetry, and a finalist in the Vernice Quebodeaux "Pathways" 2010 Poetry Prize. Plain View Press published three of her books: *Two Grains in Time, My Side of the Street*, and *Inside Out*. Her books include *White Out* (DN Publishing, 2012), *The Garbo Reels* (Pudding House Publications), *New Haven,* and *Before the Ink is Dry* (Word Tech Communications).

JAMES HARMS is the author of nine books of poetry including *Comet Scar* (Carnegie Mellon University Press 2012) and *The Only Lie Worth Telling: New and Selected Poems* (Carnegie Mellon University Press 2017). He chairs the Department of English at West Virginia University, where he teaches in the MFA Program in Creative Writing..

MARIE HARRIS was New Hampshire Poet Laureate from 1999 to 2004. She co-produced the first-ever gathering of state poets laureate. She has been a Visiting Writer at the Vermont Studio Center, where she has also been granted fellowships. She is the author of four books of poetry, including the prose poem memoir, *Your Sun, Manny* (White Pine Press, 2010) and with Kathleen Aguero is coeditor of *An Ear to the Ground: An Anthology of Contemporary American Poetry* (University of Georgia Press). Her children's books include *G is for Granite* and *Primary Numbers* (Sleeping Bear Press) and *The Girl Who Heard Colors* (A Nancy Paulsen Book; Penguin, 2013).

TODD HEARON'S first book, *Strange Land* (Southern Illinois University Press, 2010), was winner of the Crab Orchard Poetry Series Open Competition judged by former United States Poet Laureate Natasha Trethewey. Poems from *Strange Land* and from his second book, *No Other Gods* (Salmon Poetry, 2015), have appeared in literary journals such as *AGNI, Arts & Letters, Harvard Review, Ploughshares, Poetry, Poetry London*, and *Southwest Review*. Awards he has received include the PEN New England Discovery Award, the Friends of Literature Prize, a Rumi Prize in Poetry, a Dobie-Paisano Creative Writing Fellowship, and the 2014 Campbell Corner Prize. Hearon also served as the Dartmouth Poet-in-Residence at the Frost Place in Franconia, New Hampshire.

HUGH HENNEDY began writing poetry when he was fifty. In the years prior he concentrated on writing, for scholarly journals, articles on Chaucer, Shakespeare, Austen, and other English writers. A chapter from his book on Anthony Trollope, *Unity in Barsetshire*, was republished by Harold Bloom in his *Anthony Trollope's Barchester Towers and The Warden: Modern Critical Interpretations* (Chelsea House, 1988). His poems have been published in such journals as *Puckerbrush Review, Tar River Poetry*, and *James Joyce Quarterly*. His books of poetry are: *Old Winchester*

Hill (Enright House, 1993), *Halcyon Time* (Oyster River Press, 1993), *Variations on a Natural Theme* (Hobblebush Books, 2008), and *314 Franklin* (Hobblebush Books, 2010). Hennedy currently lives in Portsmouth.

KATHI HENNESSY grew up in New Hampshire and lived in Goffstown for over twenty years. She recently moved to Florida to escape the harsh northern winters. Currently employed as communications coordinator at Florida Institute of Technology, she has taught writing and literature classes and worked as a college librarian and copy editor. Her poetry has been published in dozens of journals and anthologies. While she's very happy with her new life in the Sunshine State, her heart will always reside "back home" in New Hampshire.

ELLEN HERSH'S poetry and translations have appeared in numerous publications, including *Ad Hoc Monadnock, Under the Legislature of Stars, The Other Side of Sorrow, The Eckerd Review,* and in her chapbook, *Uncapping the Chimney* (Finishing Line Press, 2014). Since 2003, she has been a member of the Skimmilk Farm Poetry Group. She holds degrees from Radcliffe College (Harvard), Yale University, and an MFA in Poetry from the Vermont College of Fine Arts. Ellen and her husband, author Burton Hersh, divide their time between Bradford, New Hampshire, where Ellen is on the roster of the New Hampshire State Council on the Arts, and St. Petersburg, Florida, where she runs poetry workshops for the Osher Lifelong Learning Institute and the Academy of Senior Professionals at Eckerd College.

DEMING HOLLERAN has been writing poems for the past twenty years. She founded an ongoing workshop, the Still Puddle Poets, with Phyllis Katz, in 1996. Thus began a joyful symbiosis with fellow poets in the Hanover area and with The Frost Place, where she attends summer conferences and has served as board chair. Deming and her husband Romer are the parents of four girls and eight grandchildren, and live with their two Cockapoo pups in Lebanon and Vero Beach, Florida. Many of her poems are rooted in a family place on an island in the St. Lawrence River.

SCOTT T. HUTCHISON has worked at Gilford High School since 1987, teaching creative writing. He has served as a director for the New Hampshire Young Writers' Conference and has been a part of the rotating faculty for the New England Young Writers' Conference.

LIN ILLINGWORTH writes and teaches writing in southern-central New Hampshire, although she lived in many cities prior to a Portsmouth visit that called her back to the New England roots planted in childhood. A student once asked her if she is a teacher-who-writes or a writer-who-teaches—a question that remains unanswered because both processes inform each other in essential ways.

GEORGE JACK was born in Cambridge, Massachusetts and has been a nearly lifelong resident of New Hampshire. He is the author of four books, *The Cellophane Tuxedo* (1998), *Frost Heaves and Flannel* (2003), *Don't Play Catch with Jelly* (Wiggles Press, 2008) and *Againaissance* (Cosmopsis Books, 2008); as well as the upcoming audio poetry collection, *Linguistininja*. His work has appeared in numerous publications, including the *National Collegiate Poetry Anthology* and *The 2008 Poet's Guide to New Hampshire*. George has been a volunteer for the Children's Poetry in the Libraries Day and a guest host at poetry readings throughout the state. He is a cast member of the New Hampshire Radio Theatre and PBSKids cartoon LunchLab; and the proud father of ten-year-old daughter, Isabella and three-year-old daughter Maddie.

MATT JASPER has had poems in *Grand Street*, *Evergreen Review*, *Fine Madness* and other magazines. His book *Moth Moon* was published by Blazevox in 2009. His work has been called "documentary surrealism" and often deals with mental illness. His band is called Pneumershonic.

MARY-CATHERINE JONES was born in Memphis, Tennessee in 1970. Her recent poetry and criticism have appeared in *Berkeley Poetry Review*, *Poetry International*, *Cultural Society*, *elimae*, *Zone 3*, *WebDelSol*, among others. She has been awarded residency by the Burnt Norton Abbey and the Apple Hill Chamber Players, in Nelson, New Hampshire. She founded and curated the Datum: Earth Reading Series / New England, since 2009. She recently moved to Portland, Oregon with her family, where she works as an associate creative director for a B-Corp advertising agency.

HOPE JORDAN'S poems have appeared in such journals as *Amoskeag*, *Many Mountains Moving*, *Green Mountains Review* and *The 2010 Poets' Guide to New Hampshire*. She was the first official poetry slam master in New Hampshire, and coached the inaugural New Hampshire Poetry Slam Team in 2007. She is the Director of Advancement for the Manchester Community Health Center.

J. KATES is a poet and literary translator who lives in Fitzwilliam, New Hampshire.

MEG KEARNEY is a novelist and poet. She has published two books of poems, *An Unkindness of Ravens* and *Home By Now*; two novels in verse for teens, *The Secret of Me* and *The Girl in the Mirror* (the third book in this trilogy will be forthcoming in 2017); and a children's picture book, *Trouper* (Scholastic, 2012), illustrated by E. B. Lewis and winner of the Kentucky Bluegrass Award. Kearney has received numerous honors for her poetry and has benefited from three residencies at the Virginia Center for the Creative Arts. She currently works as director of the low-residency Master of Fine Arts in Creative Writing program at Pine Manor College, Chestnut Hill in Massachusetts.

ALA KHAKI, a native of Mashhad, Iran, and an American by choice, has lived in the States since 1978. He began writing poetry in high school and became active in the pro-democracy movement at the age of sixteen. Arrested three times by the Shah's secret police, and imprisoned twice for activities including underground distribution of his poetry, he had to leave Iran to avoid assassination. Ala's work has been published mainly in Persian literary journals such as *Par* and *Book Review. Calling the Dawn*, a selection of his Farsi poems, was published in 1993. In 2005, he published *Return*, a selection of his English poems.

DON KIMBALL is the author of two chapbooks, *Journal of a Flatlander* (Finishing Line Press, 2009) and *Skipping Stones* (Pudding House Publications, 2008). A third chapbook, *Tumbling* (Finishing Line Press) will be released in January, 2016. His poetry has appeared in *The Formalist*, *The Lyric*, *The Blue Unicorn*, and various other journals and anthologies. Don is president of the Poetry Society of New Hampshire, and currently hosts the monthly poetry reading series at Gibson's Bookstore in Concord, New Hampshire.

LESLEY KIMBALL won an award for her contribution titled "Borderlands" to the Portsmouth Poet Laureate Program's "Voice and Vision" public art project. Her poem "Devotional" was featured by the New Hampshire Center for the Book. Her poems have appeared in *Omphalos, Salamander, Constellations, Ink-Filled Page, Café Review, Ballard Street, Foundling Review*, the anthologies *The Other Side of Sorrow* and the *2010 Poets' Guide to New Hampshire*.

ELIZABETH KNIES, a native of Pennsylvania, first came to New Hampshire in 1965. Her books and chapbooks include *The New Year & Other Poems* and *Streets after Rain* (Alice James Books); *From the Window* (Teal Press); *White Peonies* and *Going and Coming Back* (Oyster River Press). She has taught ESL, writing, critical thinking, and literature in New Hampshire, Japan, Missouri, Colorado, Maine, and Massachusetts and has worked as a journalist and an editor. She holds master's degrees from UNH and Boston University.

MAXINE KUMIN of Warner, a past New Hampshire Poet Laureate, published fifteen books of poetry, and numerous novels, essays, short stories, children's books, and more. She won many major poetry awards including (among others) the Pulitzer Prize, an Academy Arts and Letters Award, the Harvard Arts Medal in 2005, and, most recently, the prestigious Robert Frost Medal from the Poetry Society of America. Maxine served as a Consultant in Poetry to the Library of Congress and is a former Chancellor of the Academy of American Poets. She passed away on February 6, 2014.

NANCY LAGOMARSINO graduated with a BA in English from Northeastern University and an MFA in Creative Writing from Vermont College. She is the author of three books of prose poems, *Sleep Handbook* (Alice James Books, 1987), *The Secretary Parables* (Alice James Books, 1991), and *Light from an Eclipse* (White Pine Press, 2005). *Light from an Eclipse* is a memoir covering the years of her dad's Alzheimer's disease. She has lived in Hanover, New Hampshire, since 1974.

GORDON LANG was the 2011 NEATE Poet of the Year and in 2010 he was awarded the Marlon Fitzwater medallion for his work in teaching journalism. He hosts a monthly reading in the New Hampshire Lakes Region, is the treasurer of the Poetry Society of New Hampshire, and is a state advisor and local coach for Poetry Out Loud. His work has appeared in various journals, in the 2008 and 2010 volumes of *The Poets' Guide to New Hampshire*, and in the anthology *This Assignment Is So Gay*. His first book, *No Match for a Scarecrow*, is in its second edition, and his second, *Graphic Sax and Violins*, is forthcoming. He is currently editing the Poetry Society's anthology of poems titled *You Must Remember This*.

DUDLEY LAUFMAN is eighty-four years of age, was raised near Boston, and graduated from agricultural school. His poems have appeared in many magazines and journals and he has had poetry books published by William Bauhan Press, Beech River Books, and Shaker Village. Pudding House and Serif & Pixel Press published his chapbooks. He was a Pushcart Prize nominee, the recipient of the 2001 New Hampshire Governor's Arts Award in Folk Heritage, and the subject of a documentary film, *The Other Way Back*. In 2009, Dudley was honored as a National Heritage Fellow of the National Endowment for the Arts. Currently he is the honorary president of the Poetry Society of New Hampshire.

ADELLE LEIBLEIN works as a poet, artist and teacher and in recent years does much of this work at her studio in Nashua, New Hampshire. In addition to the classes and workshops offered there, she teaches at the DeCordova Museum School, the Worcester Art Museum, and through private tutorials. Her writing has been published in numerous literary magazines and anthologized in collections in China and the UK. Adelle is a founding member of Every Other Thursday, one of the longest running poets' workshops in the United States, and River Rising Poets in New Hampshire. She holds a Master's Degree from Boston University's Creative Writing Program and has held a residency at the Wurlitzer Foundation in Taos, New Mexico.

LESLE LEWIS is the author of *Small Boat*, which won the 2002 Iowa Poetry Prize, *Landscapes I & II* (Alice James Books, 2006), *lie down too* (Alice James Books 2011), and *A Boot's a Boot* (Cleveland State University Poetry Center, 2014). Her poems have appeared in many journals including the following: *Pleiades, American Letters and Commentary, Northern New England Review, Old Crow, Green Mountains Review, Barrow Street, Mudfish, Slope, LIT, Sentence*, and *Pool*. She teaches literature and writing at Landmark College in Vermont and lives in New Hampshire.

CHRISTOPHER LOCKE is the nonfiction editor for *Slice Magazine*. He has five chapbooks of poetry and has received two Dorothy Sargent Poetry Awards, and grants from the Massachusetts Cultural Council, New Hampshire Council on the Arts, and Fundacion Valparaiso (Spain). His first full-length collection of poems, *End of American Magic*, was released by Salmon Poetry in 2010. *Waiting for Grace & Other Poems* (Turning Point Books) and the collection of essays *Can I Say* (Kattywompus Press) were both released in 2013. His essay/poetry collection, *Ordinary Gods* (Salmon Poetry), and his first book for children, *The Heart Flyer* (tapStory), are forthcoming.

MAURA MACNEIL is the founder of the literary website Off the Margins (www.offthemargins.com). She is the author of the chapbook titled *A*

History of Water (Finishing Line Press, 2007) and a poetry collection titled *Lost Houses* to be published by Aldrich Press in 2016. She is a professor of creative writing and humanities and also serves as the director of the MA in Professional Writing program at New England College in Henniker, New Hampshire. She lives in Washington, New Hampshire.

RODGER MARTIN'S third poetry volume, *The Battlefield Guide* (Hobble-bush Books, 2010), uses the battlefields of the Civil War to reflect upon America today. Small Press Review selected *The Blue Moon Series* (Hobblebush Books, 2007), as its bimonthly pick of the year. A translation of his work, *On the Monadnock*, appeared in China in 2006. He received an Appalachia poetry award, a New Hampshire State Council on the Arts Fiction Fellowship, the Bruce Kellner/Monadnock Fellowship to pursue his writing, and fellowships from The National Endowment for the Humanities. In 2012 he was chosen as poet to represent the United States at Hangzhou, China's annual international cultural festival. He serves as coeditor for the Hobblebush Granite State Poetry Series and teaches journalism at Keene State College.

CLEOPATRA MATHIS'S sixth book of poems was published by Sara-bande Books in 2005. Her collection, *What to Tip the Boatman?* (Sheep Meadow Press) won the Jane Kenyon Award for Outstanding Book of Poems in 2001. Her work has appeared widely in anthologies, text-books, magazines and journals, including *The New Yorker, Poetry*, and *The Extraordinary Tide: Poetry by American Women*. Various prizes for her work include two National Endowment for the Arts grants, in 1984 and 2003; two Pushcart Prizes; the Robert Frost Award; and a 2002 Fellowship from the New Hampshire State Council on the Arts. Since 1982 she has directed the creative writing program at Dartmouth College, where she is the Frederick Sessions Beebe Professor of the Art of Writing.

GRACE MATTERN'S poems and prose have appeared in *The Sun, Prairie Schooner, Hanging Loose, Calyx*, and elsewhere. She has received fellowships from the New Hampshire State Council on the Arts and Vermont Studio Center and has published two books of poetry. *The Truth About Death* won the 2014 Readers' Choice New Hampshire Literary Award in Poetry. She has worked in the movement to end violence against women for thirty-five years. She blogs at www.gracemattern.com.

JOANNE MERRIAM is a Nova Scotian living in Nashville, who lived in New Hampshire from 2006 to 2009. She runs Upper Rubber Boot Books, which publishes science fiction and poetry from the margins. Her most recent book is *Choose Wisely: 35 Women Up To No Good*, which she co-edited with H. L. Nelson.

JENNIFER MILITELLO is the author, most recently, of *A Camouflage of Specimens and Garments* (Tupelo Press, 2016), and *Body Thesaurus* (Tupelo Press, 2013), named one of the best poetry books of 2013 by Best American Poetry. Her poems have appeared in *American Poetry Review*, *The Kenyon Review*, *The New Republic*, *The North American Review*, *The Paris Review*, and *Best New Poets*. She teaches in the MFA program at New England College.

MATT W. MILLER is the author of *Club Icarus*, winner of the 2012 Vassar Miller Poetry Prize, as well as the collection *Cameo Diner: Poems*. A former Wallace Stegner Fellow at Stanford University, his work has appeared in *Slate*, *Harvard Review*, *Notre Dame Review*, *Southwest Review*, *Florida Review*, *Third Coast*, *The Rumpus*, *Poetry Daily*, and other journals. He teaches and coaches at Phillips Exeter Academy where he also directs The Writers' Workshop at Exeter.

KATHERINE MORGAN is published in nonfiction, poetry, and fiction. Her poetry has been featured in several Plymouth Writers' Group collections, in the *Dan River Anthology*, *Piscataqua Poems*, and online. Most recently she has been an essayist and coeditor of *Beyond the Notches: Stories of Place in New Hampshire's North Country*, published by Franklin Pierce University and Bondcliff Books. She lives and writes on the seacoast of New Hampshire.

JULI NUNLIST'S first book of poetry, *Viewpoint*, was published in 2006 by Hobblebush Books. Juli, who passed away later that year, was a composer, musician and poet. A graduate of Barnard College and the Manhattan School of Music, she composed chamber music, a one-act opera and songs in three languages. The founder of the Princeton, Massachusetts Writer's Workshop, her poems were published in many journals such as *Field*, *The Comstock Review*, and *Beloit Poetry Journal*.

CATHERINE O'BRIAN lives in North Sutton, New Hampshire and works full time as Arts in Education Coordinator for the New Hampshire State Council on the Arts. She grew up in the Philippines. In 1995 she completed her MA in Writing at the University of New Hampshire. Her manuscript, *The White Nightgown*, was awarded the UNH Thomas Williams Graduate Poetry Award in 1995. Her poetry has been published in the *Red Brick Review*, *Chariton Review*, *Green Mountains Review* and other journals. In 2001 her chapbooks *Lucky to be Born in a House of Milk* and *Poems from The White Nightgown* were published by Oyster River Press as part of the Walking to Windward Series.

JULIA OLDER has lived and written in France, Italy, Mexico, Brazil, and on the Appalachian Trail, leading to her memoir *Appalachian Odyssey*. She has written thirty books as an independent writer, including the verse-novel *Tahirih Unveiled* (IPPY Bronze Poetry Medal) and a book-length poem *Tales of the François Vase* published by Hobblebush Books with a CD of her NPR play. She is editor/translator of the bilingual reader, *Boris Vian Invents Boris Vian,* published by Black Widow Press, Boston, and is finishing the final novel of her Isles of Shoals Trilogy. Her essays-stories-poems appear in *Uprooted* (Stanford Journal), *Nonbinary Review Online, The New Yorker, Poetry Loft*, and numerous other publications.

ARDELLE D. OSBORNE was born in Concord New Hampshire the daughter of a Congregational minister. She attended public schools in New England and the Rhode Island School of Design. She graduated from the Boston Museum School. She raised a son and then traveled to Europe and Greece on a scholarship. In later years, Ardelle traveled several times to Asia. She studied with Patricia Fargnoli, William Doreski and Sam Albert. Her publications include: *The Connecticut Review, Passager, Diner, Concrete Wolf* and the anthology, *Public Places.* She was a finalist in the 2008 Comstock Review contest and her winning poem was published there.

IVY PAGE writes poetry, teaches at Plymouth State University, and plants flowers like the words in her poems. Her first book, *Any Other Branch* came out in 2013; her first textbook, *Creative Writing Workshop,* was published in 2014; and her second collection of poems titled *Elemental* will be available in spring of 2016. She is currently writing her third collection of poems. Visit her site for more information: www.ivy-page.com.

PAT PARNELL of Stratham is a poet, teacher, editor, and journalist. She is author of two collections of her poetry, *Snake Woman and Other Explorations: Finding the Female in Divinity* and *Talking with Birches: Poems of Family and Everyday Life.* She serves as associate editor of *The Poets' Touchstone,* the quarterly journal of the Poetry Society of New Hampshire, and is a frequent reader and workshop participant at poetry events in the New Hampshire seacoast area.

ALEXANDRIA PEARY is the author of four books, including *Control Bird Alt Delete*, winner of the 2013 Iowa Poetry Prize. Her poetry and non-fiction have appeared in journals including *New England Review, Denver Quarterly, Volt, North American Review, Massachusetts Review, Gettysburg Review, Crazyhorse,* and *Hotel Amerika*. Her work has been awarded the Joseph Langland Award from the Academy of American Poets. She is an associate professor in the English Department at Salem State University.

ANDREW C. PERIALE is an Emmy-nominated artist and has toured throughout the United States as an actor and puppeteer. He's been the editor of *Puppetry International* for thirty years and has written plays that have been performed all over the country. His poetry has appeared in *Light Quarterly, Yellow Medicine Review, Entelechy International, Burnt Bridge,* and others. A member of City Hall Poets (Portsmouth, New Hampshire), he also served for four years as the Poet Laureate of Rochester. He is currently touring a one-man show called "Mano-a-Monolog."

JOHN PERRAULT is the author of *Jefferson's Dream* (Hobblebush Books, 2009), *Here Comes the Old Man Now* (Oyster River Press, 2005), and *The Ballad of Louis Wagner* (Peter Randall Publisher, 2003). He has recorded nine albums of original ballads and songs. His CD *Rough Cuts* was a finalist in the 1989 Crossroads Music Magazine Awards, and his latest compilation, "Rock and Root" is available from CD Baby. John's poetry has appeared in the *Salmon Poetry Anthology, Dogs Singing, The Christian Science Monitor, Commonweal, Poet Lore,* and elsewhere. John was poet laureate of Portsmouth, New Hampshire from 2003 to 2005. www.johnperrault.com

MEG J. PETERSEN is the director of the National Writing Project in New Hampshire, and a professor of English at Plymouth State University. Her poetry has appeared in *Concrete Wolf, Entelechy International: A Journal of Contemporary Ideas, Garden Lane, English Journal, The International Journal for Teaching Writing,* and other publications. In 1997, she was named New England Poet of the Year by the New England Association of Teachers of English. Her poem, "Bringing Down the Ceiling" was featured in a poetry month display at the New Hope Gallery in Bristol, Rhode Island. Her poetry has also appeared in the anthologies *The Why and Later* and *No Regrets*.

PATRICE PINETTE, inspired by alchemy between the arts, dances as well as writes poems, and creates poetry-pastels exhibited with the Visual Poetry Collective. Her poems have appeared in *The Inflectionist Review, Evening Street Review, Northern New England Review, Adanna,*

Poetica, Connecticut River Review, and *Smoky Quartz,* among others. A teacher and tutor, she loves writing with teenagers, leads workshops for adults, and is an adjunct at Antioch University New England. She received her MFA in Writing from Vermont College of Fine Arts.

KYLE POTVIN'S first poetry collection, *Sound Travels on Water* (Finishing Line Press), was co-winner of New England Poetry Club's 2014 Jean Pedrick Chapbook Award. She was named a finalist for the 2008 Howard Nemerov Sonnet Award. Her poetry has appeared in *The New York Times, Measure, The Huffington Post, JAMA,* among others. She is on the board of the Poetry Society of New Hampshire and helps coordinate the Robert Frost Farm's Hyla Brook Reading Series.

CHARLES W. PRATT attended Phillips Exeter Academy and then returned there to teach in the 1960s. In the early 1980s, he and his wife Joan bought an apple orchard in nearby Brentwood, which they operated until 2011. The central poems of his first book, *In the Orchard* (Tidal Press, 1986) were written with the encouragement of a grant from the New Hampshire State Council on the Arts; his chapbook *Still Here* (Finishing Line Press) followed in 2008. *From the Box Marked Some are Missing* became the first volume in the Hobblebush Granite State Poetry Series in 2010. Charlie died in 2012. His memorial service at Phillips Church in Exeter was attended by over 500 people and was designed around his poems.

JAMES RIOUX studied poetry at the University of New Hampshire and Georgia State University, where he received the Gerard Manley Hopkins Award. His work has appeared in a variety of publications including *Five Points, Agenda, The North American Review, The Cafe Review, Ars Interpres,* and *Prairie Schooner.* His first book, *Fistfuls of the Invisible,* was published by Penhallow Press. He currently teaches writing at the University of New Hampshire.

BECKY DENNISON SAKELLARIOU, born and raised in New England, has lived most of her adult life in Greece, the Balkans, and the Mediterranean region, working as a teacher, counselor and editor. She has published in numerous journals over the past twenty years, been nominated twice for the Pushcart Prize, and has published four books: *The Importance of Bone* (Blue Light Press, 2005), *Earth Listening* (Hobblebush Books, 2010), *What Shall I Cry?* (Finishing Line Press, 2013) and *The Possibility of Red,* a bilingual selection in English and Greek (Hobblebush Books, 2014). Becky can be found either in Peterborough, New Hampshire, or in Euboia, Greece. www.beckysakellariou.com.

FRED SAMUELS grew up in Brooklyn, New York, but was always a country boy at heart. After teaching Sociology and Race Relations at University of New Hampshire for twenty-seven years, he retired to Alton, New Hampshire. He was a longtime officer of the Poetry Society of New Hampshire, and though shy by nature, he attended many open-mic venues. In addition to his many writings in the field of Sociology, his publications included *To Spade the Earth and Other Poems* and *Breakfast in the Bathtub: A Book of Smiles*, co-authored with Joann Duncanson. In December, 2008, while driving home through an ice storm, his car skidded off the road and into a tree, thus beginning a period of failing health. Fred Samuels died on June 16, 2009.

CHERYL SAVAGEAU, an Abenaki poet, has been awarded fellowships in poetry from the National Endowment for the Arts and the Massachusetts Artists Foundation, and three residencies at the MacDowell Colony. Her second book of poetry, *Dirt Road Home*, was a finalist for the Paterson Poetry Prize. She was awarded Mentor of the Year by Wordcraft Circle of Native Writers and Storytellers, as well as Writer of the Year for her children's book, *Muskrat Will Be Swimming*. Savageau's third collection of poetry, *Mother/Land*, was published by Salt Publishing as part of their Earthworks series in 2006. Her poetry has been widely anthologized, most recently in *French Connections* and *The Eye of the Deer*.

HARVEY SHEPARD'S poetry has appeared in *Poetry East*, *Poet Lore*, *The Texas Observer*, *In Posse Review*, *Sol Poetry Daily*, *The Connecticut River Review*, *Roanoke Review*, and other journals and anthologies. He also has written book reviews and opinion pieces for *The Philadelphia Inquirer* and other publications. He has served on several nonprofit boards, including the Portsmouth Poet Laureate Program, and is a past president of the Seacoast Jazz Society. He is professor emeritus of physics at the University of New Hampshire in Durham, New Hampshire. Harvey was born in Chicago, spent the '60s in southern California, and has lived in New Hampshire for more than thirty-five years. hshepard@gmail.com

RALPH SNEEDEN'S poems and essays have appeared or are forthcoming in *AGNI*, *The American Poetry Review*, *The Common*, *Ecotone*, *Harvard Review*, *The Kenyon Review*, *New England Review*, *Ploughshares*, *The New Republic*, *Slate* and others. His new manuscript, *Barcarole*, was a finalist for the National Poetry Series, the Lena-Miles Wever Todd Prize and the May Swenson Poetry Award. The title poem of his first book, *Evidence of the Journey*, received the Friends of Literature Prize from

Poetry Magazine. He was born in Los Angeles and has been teaching at Phillips Exeter Academy since 1995.

BETSY SNIDER is a retired attorney who lives on a lake in Acworth with her cat, Sophie, and the ghosts of her many dogs. When she is not swimming or hiking, she writes poetry and has volunteered as a CASA Guardian ad Litem for abused and neglected children. Her poetry has been published in a variety of journals and anthologies, most recently, *River of Earth and Sky: Poems for the 21st Century* and *Love Over 60: An Anthology of Women Poets*. She also contributed to the groundbreaking *Lesbian Nuns: Breaking Silence*. She is also the winner of the 2015 Blue Light Book Award for her collection, *Hope is a Muscle*.

KATHERINE SOLOMON has an MFA in Writing from Vermont College and has taught at the New Hampshire Community Technical College in Claremont. Her poems have appeared in various reviews including, *Naugatuck River Review, Green Mountains Review, Worcester Review, Spoon River Poetry Review,* and in several anthologies, including the upcoming, *Far Out: Poems of the Sixties*. She is a recipient of an Individual Fellowship from the New Hampshire State Council on the Arts, and has two chapbooks, *Tempting Fate* from Oyster River Press and *Transit of Venus* from Finishing Line Press.

S STEPHANIE'S poetry, fiction, and book reviews have appeared in many literary magazines, such as *Birmingham Poetry Review, Café Review, Cease, Cows, Literary Laundry, OVS, Rattle, St. Petersburg Review, Solidus, Southern Indiana Review, The Southern Review, The Sun,* and *Third Coast*. She has three published collections of poetry. She holds an MFA from Vermont College of Fine Art and is an adjunct instructor at the New Hampshire Institute of Art in Manchester, New Hampshire.

NANCY STEWART grew up in Concord, spent some time at UNH, six years in San Francisco, and the last twenty-five with her husband in their sandwich shop in Concord. Her poems have appeared in *Bone and Flesh*, No. 16, and in the Seacoast Writers Association's *Currents V*. She is a member of Concord's Yogurt Poets and a past member of Portsmouth City Hall Poets. She lives in Pembroke with her husband and their grown daughter's cat.

MARY ANN SULLIVAN has an MFA in Writing from Vermont College of Norwich University and a Doctor of Arts degree from Franklin Pierce

University. As a cloistered Cistercian and later Dominican nun, Mary Ann wrote poetry using a monastic practice called lectio divina. That poetry appears in her e-chapbook *Mending My Black Sweater* (eratio Editions). Her poems have been published online at places such as *BBC Arts Online* and *BlazeVox*. Her literary interviews and commentaries appear in sites like *Jacket* and in The Poetry Library at the Southbank Centre, London. Mary Ann teaches writing at St. Joseph School of Nursing, Southern New Hampshire University, and Great Bay Community College. She is the editor of *The Tower Journal* and enjoys lecturing on the topic of digital poetry.

JANET SYLVESTER'S poetry publications include *That Mulberry Wine* (Wesleyan University Press), *The Mark of Flesh* (W.W. Norton) and her new book (under consideration by several publishers), *Breakwater*. Her collector's edition chapbook, *A Visitor at the Gate*, was hand-printed and bound by Shinola Press. Sylvester's poems have appeared in many journals and anthologies, including *The Best American Poetry, Triquarterly, Harvard Review, Virginia Quarterly Review*, and *Poetry Daily*. She is a recipient of the Grolier Poetry Prize, a Pen Discovery Award and a Pushcart Prize and has been awarded multiple fellowships to the MacDowell Colony, Yaddo and others. She directs the low-residency BFA in Creative Writing Program at Goddard College in Vermont.

MAREN C. TIRABASSI is the author of nineteen books, including the recent *From the Psalms to the Cloud* with Maria Mankin, and the Lambda Award nominated *Transgendering Faith—Identity, Sexuality, and Spirituality* with Leanne McCall Tigert, both published by The Pilgrim Press. Fiction, new in 2014, is *The Shakespeare Reader and Other Christmas Tales*. She maintains the global poetry and liturgy blog *Gifts in Open Hands* at: www.giftsinopenhands.wordpress.com. A past Poet Laureate of Portsmouth, New Hampshire, she is pastor of Madbury United Church of Christ and leads workshops on writing and ministry in a wide range of settings.

PARKER TOWLE is the author of five poetry collections, the last two, full-length, from Antrim House Books: *This Weather is No Womb* (2007), and *World Spread Out* (2015). He co-authored *Poems and Collage* (2013), with the collagist, Barbara Newton. He is an associate editor at *The Worcester Review* and has edited special issues for them on Frank O'Hara and Stanley Kunitz. For twenty-five years he was on the board of the Frost Place in Franconia, New Hampshire, and taught at its summer festival.

KATIE UMANS' first collection of poems, *Flock Book*, was published by Black Lawrence Press in 2012. Her writing has appeared in *Prairie Schooner, Los Angeles Review, Crazyhorse, Columbia, Indiana Review, Barrow Street*, and others. She has an MFA from the University of Michigan and has received support from the Wisconsin Institute for Creative Writing and the New Hampshire State Council on the Arts. She is currently the assistant director of the University of New Hampshire's Center for the Humanities.

DIANALEE VELIE lives and writes in Newbury, New Hampshire. She is a graduate of Sarah Lawrence College and has an MFA in Writing from Manhattanville College where she served as a faculty advisor of *Inkwell: A Literary Magazine*. She has taught poetry, memoir, and short story at universities and colleges in several states and in private workshops throughout the United States, Canada and Europe. Her award-winning poetry and short stories have been published in hundreds of literary journals and many have been translated into Italian. She is the author of four books of poetry and one collection of short stories.

ROBERTA VISSER leads poetry workshops for elementary through high school students in libraries, after-school programs, and through college continuing education courses. Most recently her poems have been published in *The Worcester Review, Entelechy International, Late Blooms Poetry Postcard Series*, and *damselfly press*. She has also been a contributing writer for the "Monadnock Living" page of the daily *Keene Sentinel*. She is the author of a chapbook titled, *Listen to Me*, and a second chapbook, *birds are calling, Elov! Elov!* from which this poem is taken.

CHRISTOPHER VOLPE grew up in Oyster Bay, Long Island, New York. He wrote and studied poetry for some fifteen years before enrolling in UNH's master's program to study with Charles Simic. After graduate school, he worked in journalism and public relations until a stint teaching art history gradually seduced him into becoming, at the age of 41, a full-time oil painter and art writer. While painting has replaced poetry as primary medium, the objective remains the expression of deeply embedded individual and universal experiences of reality. www.christophervolpe.com and www.christophervolpe.blogspot.com

DORINDA WEGENER co-founded Trio House Press, a nonprofit publisher of distinct voices in American poetry, where she currently serves as president and managing editor. A Joel Oppenheimer Award recipient, her work has appeared in *The Antioch Review, Indiana Review, Hotel Amerika, Mid-American Review, Hinchas de Poesia, THRUSH Poetry Journal*, and elsewhere, as well as anthologized in *Knocking at the Door* (Birch Bench Press, an imprint of Write Bloody Publishing). She has resided in Robert Frost's first New Hampshire home prior to his famous farm.

DONALD WELLMAN is a poet and translator. His books include *The Cranberry Series* and *A North Atlantic Wall* (both from Dos Madres) and *Prolog Pages* (Ahadada). His *Roman Exercises* was released by Talisman House (fall 2015). He edited the O.ARS series of anthologies exploring postmodern and experimental poetics. He writes on contemporary poetry and poetics. He translates from both German and Spanish. Recent books of poetry in translation feature work by Antonio Gamoneda and Emilio Prados. His translation from the German of Neila's *Evening Song: Last Poems of Yvan Goll* was published by Spuyten Duyvil (2015). A bilingual anthology and critical assessment of Wellman's work, *Remando de Noche*, is available from the University of Valencia (2015).

CAROL WESTBERG'S *Terra Infirma* was a finalist for the 2014 Tampa Review Prize for Poetry, and *Slipstream* was a finalist for the New Hampshire Literary Award for Outstanding Book of Poetry. Her poems have appeared in *Prairie Schooner, Hunger Mountain*, and *North American Review*, among other journals, and she was recently interviewed on NHPR's *All Things Considered*. Carol earned degrees from Duke (BA), Stanford (MAT), and Vermont College (MFA) and lives in Hanover, New Hampshire. www.carolwestberg.com

MIMI WHITE is the author of three collections of poetry: *The Singed Horizon*, winner of the Philbrick Award; *The Last Island,* winner of the Jane Kenyon Award for Outstanding Poetry; and *Memory Won't Save Me*, a haibun, nominated for a Pushcart. Her most recent collection is *The World Disguised as This One: A Year in Tanka* (Deerbrook Editions, 2015).

SARA WILLINGHAM lives and writes in Concord, New Hampshire. Her poems have been published in a variety of literary journals and magazines, including *Poetry East, SRPR (Spoon River Poetry Review), Southern Poetry Review, Lullwater Review, Nimrod* and several others. Sara is a member of the New Hampshire Writers Project and a former poetry editor for *The Granite Review*. She has performed in readings throughout the region and has had the opportunity to study in master workshops with many remarkable New England poets. Sara is also a fine-arts photographer and often incorporates visual imagery from her photographs into her poems.

CREDITS

"A Dictionary at the Turn of the Millennium" by Jennifer Militello. Originally appeared in *Crazyhorse*. Reprinted by permission of the author.

"A Wooden Horse" from *Comet Scar*. © 2012 by James Harms. Reprinted by permission of Carnegie Mellon University Press, www.cmu.edu/universitypress.

"April 1918" from *Blood Garden: An Elegy for Raymond* by Pamela Bernard. © 2010 by Pamela Bernard. Reprinted by permission of WordTech Communications LLC.

"Artist Undefiled" by Linda Dyer. Originally appeared in *Birmingham Poetry Review*. Reprinted by permission of the author.

"At the Home" from *Here Comes The Old Man Now* by John Perrault. © 2005 by John Perrault. Reprinted by permission of Oyster River Press.

"Ballistics" from *Club Icarus* by Matt Miller. © 2013 by Matt Miller. Reprinted by permission of University of North Texas Press.

"Book Burning" from *Tahirih Unveiled* by Julia Older. © 2007 by Julia Older. Reprinted by permission of the author.

"Bringing Down the Ceiling" by Meg Petersen. Originally appeared in *Concrete Wolf*. © 2001 by Meg Petersen. Reprinted by permission of the author.

"Cadenza" by Lisa Bourbeau. Originally appeared in *First Intensity*, No. 22. © 2007 by Lisa Bourbeau. Reprinted by permission of the author.

"Calling to the Soul of My Unborn Child" by Adelle Leiblein. Previously appeared in *Anthology of Birth Poetry*, Virago Press, UK. Reprinted by permission of the author.

"Canis" from *Book of Dog* by Cleopatra Mathis. © 2012 by Cleopatra Mathis. Reprinted by permission of Sarabande Books.

"Circling" from *The Truth About Death* by Grace Mattern. © 2012 by Turning Point Books. Reprinted by permission of Turning Point Books, Cincinnati, Ohio.

"Cow's Neck" from *Evidence of the Journey* by Ralph Sneeden. © 2007 by Ralph Sneeden. Reprinted by permission of Harmon Blunt Publishers.

"Deer in a Craft Shop" by Don Kimball. Originally appeared in *Schuylkill Valley Journal of the Arts*. Reprinted by permission of the author.

"Dos Equis" from *Graphic Sax and Violins* by Gordon Lang. © 2015 by Aisling Sweet Dreams. Reprinted by permission of Aisling Sweet Dreams.

"Ekphrastics" from *Flock Book* by Katie Umans. © 2012 by Katie Umans. Reprinted by permission of Black Lawrence Press.

"Fallen Snow" from *Mary Lou: The Persistence of Memory* by Don Burness. © 2011 by Don Burness. Reprinted by permission of Twenty-three Books.

Index of Poets

About the Editors

ALICE B. FOGEL is the poet laureate of New Hampshire. Her newest poetry collection, *Interval: Poems Based on Bach's "Goldberg Variations,"* won the Nicholas Schaffner Award for Music in Literature. Her third book, *Be That Empty,* was a national poetry bestseller, and she is also the author of the guide for readers and teachers, *Strange Terrain,* on how to appreciate poetry without necessarily "getting" it. Nominated seven times for the Pushcart Prize, Fogel's poems have appeared in many journals and anthologies, including *Best American Poetry,* Robert Hass's *Poet's Choice, Yale Letters, Inflectionist Review, Spillway, Hotel Amerika,* and *Upstairs at Duroc,* an international arts journal based out of Paris. She has received a fellowship from the National Endowment for the Arts, among other awards.

SIDNEY HALL, JR. was born in 1951 and has lived most of his life in southern New Hampshire. He is a graduate of Reed College, where he studied Greek and Latin Classics. He is the founder and owner of Hobblebush Books. He is also the owner of Hobblebush Design, which specializes in book design and production for other publishers.

His poems have appeared in the *Graham House Review, Chattahoochie Review, Hampden-Sydney Poetry Review, Wisconsin Review, California Quarterly, Hollins Critic,* the *Los Angeles Times Book Review,* and other magazines and journals, as well as on Garrison Keillor's *Writer's Almanac* and in several poetry anthologies. His book reviews have also appeared in the *Los Angeles Times Book Review.* He is the author of three books of poems, *What We Will Give Each Other, Chebeague,* and *Fumbling in the Light,* and a book of memoirs, *Small Town Tales,* a collection of his newspaper columns.